OSPREY COMBAT AIRCRAFT • 96

Pe-2 GUARDS UNITS OF WORLD WAR 2

SERIES EDITOR: TONY HOLMES

OSPREY COMBAT AIRCRAFT • 96

Pe-2 GUARDS UNITS OF WORLD WAR 2

DMITRIY KHAZANOV AND ALEKSANDER MEDVED

OSPREY
PUBLISHING

Front Cover
In early July 1944 Soviet intelligence detected a large warship in the Finnish port of Kotka. It was erroneously identified as the coastal defence ship *Vainamoinen*, the largest warship in the Finnish Navy. In reality this vessel was the 6000-tonne German heavy anti-aircraft depot ship *Niobe*, formerly the Dutch coastal defence destroyer *Gelderland*, which was similar in appearance and displacement to the *Vainamoinen*. Following instructions from the People's Commissariat of the Navy, Adm N G Kuznetsov, preparations began for a simultaneous mass assault on the ship led by Gen M I Samokhin of the Red Banner Air Forces of the Baltic Fleet.

This was to be an assault by four air groups, consisting of 133 aircraft, and they were to all carry out their bombing runs within a narrow seven-minute window. The aircraft were divided into specific groups, with some suppressing flak batteries and others acting as decoys. There would also be a powerful fighter presence. The principal task of sinking the ship was assigned to 24 Pe-2s (led by 12th GvBAP CO Maj V I Rakov in the aircraft depicted in this artwork) and four A-20Gs (led by Maj I N Ponomarenko).

The mission was duly executed on the afternoon of 16 July, with its principal goal being accomplished. There was a large explosion aboard the *Niobe* (which was hit by as many as ten large bombs), after which a huge column of black smoke began to rise from the stricken vessel. According to reports from returning bomber crews, the vessel broke up and sank. This was not confirmed in German documentation from the period, however.

Soon after he had returned from the mission, Maj Rakov was promoted to the rank of colonel. By war's end he had flown 172 combat sorties, of which around 100 were in the Pe-2, and participated in the sinking of 12 ships. Rakov was the first aviator in both 12th GvBAP and the Red Banner Air Forces of the Baltic Fleet to have been twice awarded the title of Hero of the Soviet Union. Rakov recalled the following details of the *Niobe* mission.

The aviation group allocated for the strike on the "cruiser" consisted of 133 aircraft, all of which were to concentrate over the target in just five to seven minutes. This mass attack would force the enemy anti-aircraft

artillery to fire in different directions at different altitudes. According to the plan, three squadrons of dive-bombers were to approach the target from three different directions. Within the squadrons aircraft were split into wings, each of them attacking from a different altitude. 'At 1652 hrs the first bombs started to fall on Niobe. After approaching from an altitude of 3000 metres, and following a 40-degree turn, the Pe-2s commenced their diving runs on the vessel from a height of 2000 metres. The first wing managed to hit the "cruiser", which it

left engulfed in smoke. The pilots of ground attack aircraft in the immediate vicinity saw two direct hits by 250-kg bombs dropped from the Pe-2s. The exact number of hits obtained was difficult to gauge due to the fire and heavy smoke that enveloped the vessel. According to enemy records that were subsequently captured, the ship received more than ten direct hits. Many bombs also exploded near the hull, which also inflicted damage on the vessel' (*Cover artwork by Mark Postlethwaite*)

First published in Great Britain in 2013 by Osprey Publishing
Midland House, West Way, Botley, Oxford, OX2 0PH
43-01 21st Street, Suite 220B, Long Island City, NY 11101, USA

E-mail; info@ospreypublishing.com

Osprey Publishing is part of the Osprey Group

A CIP catalogue record for this book is available from the British Library

ISBN: 978 1 78096 065 4
PDF e-book ISBN: 978 1 78096 066 1
e-Pub ISBN: 978 1 78096 067 8

Edited by Tony Holmes and Phil Jarrett
Cover Artwork by Mark Postlethwaite
Aircraft Profiles and Scale Drawings by Andrey Yurgenson
Index by Alan Thatcher
Originated by PDQ Media, Bungay, UK
Printed in China through Bookbuilders

13 14 15 16 17   10 9 8 7 6 5 4 3 2 1

Osprey Publishing is supporting the Woodland Trust, the UK's leading woodland conservation charity, by funding the dedication of trees.

www.ospreypublishing.com

CONTENTS

CHAPTER ONE

Pe-2 DEVELOPMENT 6

CHAPTER TWO

GUARDS BOMBER AIR REGIMENTS 13

CHAPTER THREE

GUARDS BOMBER AIR DIVISIONS 30

CHAPTER FOUR

GUARDS BOMBER AIR CORPS 53

CHAPTER FIVE

**GUARDS RECONNAISSANCE
AIR REGIMENTS 66**

CHAPTER SIX

**GUARDS BOMBER AIR REGIMENTS
OF NAVAL AIR FORCES 82**

APPENDICES 90
COLOUR PLATES COMMENTARY 91
INDEX 96

Pe-2 DEVELOPMENT

In the summer of 1937 the abbreviation 'ANT', denoting aircraft designed by Soviet designer Andrei Nikolayevich Tupolev, was seen as a symbol of success around the world. On 20 June that year an ANT-25, piloted by V P Chkalov, landed in the USA, followed on 15 July by a second such aircraft piloted by M M Gromov, which set a world record for long-range flight. At that time another of Tupolev's aircraft was becoming 'widely known' by combatants in China and Spain, the high-speed ANT-40 (SB) bomber.

Everything seemed to be developing well for Tupolev and his design collective, and he could rely wholly on support from both the leadership of the Soviet aviation industry and from the state. However, in the notorious atmosphere of 1937 things were happening that were very hard to explain. In the evening of 21 October three men entered the office of chief designer Tupolev, while a fourth sat on a chair next to his secretary and suggested that she did not answer any telephone calls and did not go out. A tired Andrei Tupolev emerged into the reception room at 0300 hrs the next morning, surrounded by his 'visitors'.

After holding out for a week, on 28 October Tupolev signed a statement in which he acknowledged that he had formed an anti-Soviet group made up of his colleagues and subordinates (indicating their names), which was engaged in sabotage and subversive activity. One of the members of the 'anti-Soviet group', Vladimir Petlyakov, head of the Heavy Aircraft Brigade, was arrested the following day. He resisted for three days, but on 1 November, under pressure from the investigators, he acknowledged his 'crimes'. These dramatic events became the main reason behind the emergence of the most mass-produced Soviet twin-engined aeroplane of all time, the Pe-2 dive-bomber.

In the summer of 1938 a Special Technical Department (STO) for aviation was formed within the structure of the People's Commissariat of Internal Affairs (NKVD). V M Petlyakov's group turned out to be the first design collective in the STO. While still in the special prison located not far from the railway station at Bolshevo, in the Moscow region,

The first series production Pe-2, which was built at Moscow Factory No 39. The navigator's canopy includes the so-called 'turtle' section that could be lowered

Petlyakov proposed the design and manufacture of a twin-engined high-altitude fighter with a pressure cabin and turbo-supercharged engines. Since the acronym 'STO' sounds similar to the figure '100' in Russian, the aircraft was later nicknamed 'Sotka' (100).

According to performance estimates the aircraft's ceiling was to be 12,500 m (41,000 ft), and its maximum speed was to be 630 km/h (390 mph) at an altitude of 10,000 m (32,800 ft). The prototype had to be ready for its first flight before the end of 1939, and this tight schedule gave rise to the introduction of an 11-hour working day without breaks for the workers in the 'sharashka' (an informal name given to the secret research and development laboratories established within the Soviet Gulag labour camp system). The first full-scale mock-up of the new aircraft was completed in May 1939, and the 'Sotka' completed its maiden flight on 22 December 1939.

The '100, with twin M-105 engines, twin TK-2 turbo-superchargers and two pressure cabins', was considered innovative in the Soviet Union, despite its wholly traditional layout. Two of the most modern M-105 engines (the VK-105 was a Hispano-Suiza 12Y variant built under licence by V Ya Klimov), driving VISh-42 propellers, were installed in the aircraft, and their TK-2 turbo-superchargers were incorporated into the structure of the engine nacelles. The crew of three was accommodated in two pressure cabins fed by compressed air from the turbo-superchargers that supported normal pressure up to an altitude of 10,000 metres (32,800 ft).

Offensive armament included two 20 mm ShVAK cannon and two 7.62 mm ShKAS machine guns. A fixed ShKAS machine gun was also installed in the aircraft's tailcone to protect the fighter against attacks from the rear. The option of suspending two 250- or 500-kg bombs on external bomb racks was explored for the fighter-bomber variant.

On the morning of 1 May 1940 Maj Stefanovskiy demonstrated the aircraft publicly during the commemorative aviation parade in Moscow. Petlyakov and his colleagues watched the flight from the roof of their prison.

Despite the defects that had come to light during the preliminary trials, the general conclusion on testing the '100' aircraft was favourable. It was noted that 'the "100" represents the most successful solution to the problems of creating an aircraft with a pressurised cabin. It is considered expedient to create a dive-bomber variant without a pressurised cabin on the basis of the "100" aircraft, with the aim of using its good aerodynamics. A trial series of aircraft must be manufactured'.

The third point raised following the preliminary trials ultimately affected the fate of the 'Sotka', as it stated that the threat posed by high-altitude bombers was thought to be exaggerated. In reality, the few high-altitude aircraft the Germans possessed – the Junkers Ju 86P and Ju 86R and the Henschel Hs 130 – were principally used for strategic reconnaissance. At that time, right at the outbreak of World War 2, German Junkers Ju 87 dive-bombers were really making their mark, becoming a real curse for both land forces and naval fleets among Germany's enemies.

The idea of a dive-bomber was not new, but the results achieved by the Stukas in 1939-40 turned out to be revelatory for air arms across the globe. And highly effective bombing by Ju 87s was, quite rightly, a serious concern for the leadership of the USSR.

The ability to carry a 1000-kg total bomb load was particularly underlined in the conclusion to the testing of the '100'. The change in the 'Sotka's' role was supported by the fact that it already boasted many of the features of a dive-bomber. For example, it had good stability in a dive and was sufficiently strong enough to withstand the stresses and strains associated with such a flight regime. On 23 June 1940 the Committee for Defence received a decree ordering the commencement of series production of the dive-bomber variant of the '100' at Moscow aviation plants Nos 22 and 39.

The dive-bomber (designated the PB-100) was expected to achieve a maximum speed of 535 km/h at an altitude of 4800-4900 m (330 mph at 15,750-16,000 ft). It was to have a range of 1600 km at an altitude of 5000 metres (1000 miles at 16,400 ft), having taken into account the amount of fuel consumed when taxiing, during takeoff and initial climb-out. The ceiling for the PB-100 was set at 8000 metres (26,250 ft).

Petlyakov and his collective were given just 45 days for a major redesign of their high-altitude fighter, requiring the development and testing of a practically new fuselage incorporating airbrake panels and their control systems, a fundamental review of crew accommodation and a change of the engine/propeller unit. Static tests were carried out only in relation to the new components – the fuselage with its large blisters in the tail section and the new engine nacelles. Drawings were prepared within the timescale. The promise given to Petlyakov and some of his colleagues by the dreaded chief of the NKVD, Lavrentiy Beria, that 'if the aircraft flies, you go free', was kept.

When compared with the '100' high-altitude fighter, the dive-bomber's appearance had changed considerably. The navigator was now seated with the pilot in a shared, unpressurised cabin, and was given a defensive ShKAS machine gun in a TSS-1 turret. The gunner's position was fitted with a hatch installation and another ShKAS machine gun. The pilot could open fire with two fixed ShKAS machine guns mounted in the nose cone. Other differences principally concerned the engine/propeller unit, the turbo-superchargers having been removed, the shape of the oil-cooler tunnels changed and the radiator surface area increased.

On 15 December 1940 the test pilot of Factory No 39, N Fedorov, took aircraft 390101 (the lead machine of the first series) aloft. The designation Pe-2 was adopted in accordance with new rules introduced that same month, which stipulated that the first two letters of an aircraft's designation were to be the first letters of the chief designer's surname.

With a takeoff weight of 6800 kg (14,990 lbs), the Pe-2 developed a maximum speed of 540 km/h (335 mph) at an altitude of 5000 metres (16,400 ft), which corresponded fully with the technical proposal laid out in the dive-bomber decree that had been issued to Petlyakov. An altitude of 5000 metres was reached in 9.2 minutes with a 600 kg (1320-

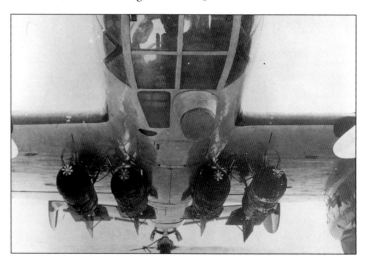

When used as a dive-bomber, the Pe-2 could carry up to four FAB-250 bombs on external mounts. Extensive nose glazing gave the crew a good field of view

lb) bomb load on internal bomb racks, and the ceiling was 8800 metres (28,870 ft). The aircraft was deemed to be a success thanks to its flight performance characteristics, and there were no serious in-flight incidents during state trials at the Air Force Scientific Testing Institute.

In February 1941 series production of the Pe-2 commenced at aircraft plants Nos 124 (Kazan) and 125 (Irkutsk). It was hoped that 525 dive-bombers could be built in the first six months of 1941, but according to reports from the factories only 458 machines were delivered.

The German invasion of the Soviet Union in June 1941 soon put the Pe-2 to the test, and the combat experience gleaned by frontline units accelerated the process of refining the machine many times over. A series of changes to assemblies and subassemblies was hastily introduced, the first and foremost of these centring on increased weaponry in an attempt to improve the aircraft's survivability. One of the pilot's forward ShKAS machine guns was replaced by a 12.7 mm BK weapon, and a 12.7 mm UBT machine gun in an MB-2 turret was mounted in the hatch installation in the radio-operator/gunner's position.

By the end of 1941 another ShKAS machine gun had been fitted to the 'Peshka', as the Pe-2 was nicknamed in frontline service. Attached to one of two spherical mountings at the radio-operator/gunner position, the weapon could be moved from side to side. The radio-operator/gunner could fire the ShKAS into the upper hemisphere through the upper hatch by simply holding it in his hands.

Other changes introduced at this time included the strengthening of armour plating around the navigator and radio-operator/gunner and the removal of vulnerable service tanks from the engine nacelles. The tanks' design, along with the system by which they were filled with inert gas as they emptied, was also improved. Aside from the introduction of qualitative improvements, production of the 'Peshkas' was also increased across all the aircraft plants that had been mobilised. Consequently, the industry produced 239 Pe-2s in July 1941 and 295 the following month.

Moscow was subjected to German air raids from the end of July 1941, and three newly completed Pe-2s manufactured at Factory No 22 were set on fire on the airfield at Tushino at this time. The other Moscow plant, No 39, which predominantly produced the Pe-3 nightfighter version of the Pe-2, was evacuated to Irkutsk, where it was soon merged with Factory No 125. Factory No 22 was also relocated at the same time, being moved to Kazan. It had been 'swallowed' by the local Factory No 124 by the end of the year. V M Petlyakov's design bureau also moved to Kazan. Naturally, the evacuation led to a reduction in the number of dive-bombers produced. Nevertheless, in 1941 the four plants engaged in series production manufactured 1671 dive-bombers and 196 fighters, enabling many operational units along the length of the Soviet-German Front to be equipped with 'Peshkas'.

In January 1942 chief designer V M Petlyakov was killed in a flying accident. His successors elected to continue development of the 'Peshka' and changes were introduced, while keeping their effect on output to a minimum. Combat had quickly shown that the Pe-2's Achilles' heel was the ineffectiveness of the navigator's ShKAS machine gun, which defended the upper hemisphere to the rear of the bomber. A group of designers at Factory No 22, led by L L Selyakov, found a successful compromise solution in the form of a new 'FT' upper pivot assembly fitted with a 12.7 mm UBT machine gun.

In order to improve the Pe-2's ability to protect itself from fighter attacks from the upper rear area, the ShKAS 7.62 mm machine gun in the navigator's turret was replaced by a 12.7 mm UBT high-calibre weapon. Unofficially, this version was designated Pe-2FT (for 'Front Trebuet' – front demands)

Its principal advantage was that it was easily fitted. The introduction of the 'FT' had almost no effect on the number of aircraft produced. However, the lack of a cowling to keep out the worst of the weather made the navigator's working conditions even more severe than they already were.

A more fundamental change in the Pe-2's design from the 110 series onwards was the introduction of the new VUB-1 glazed turret fitted with a UBT machine gun and continuous belt feed in June 1942. Compared with the 'FT', the VUB-1 gave greater firing angles and improved working conditions for the crew. This variant is often mistakenly described in the west as the 'Pe-2FT'.

The 'Peshka' would also benefit from the work undertaken by the V Ya Klimov design bureau in 1942, its efforts focusing on augmenting the M-105P and M-105R engines by increasing their boost up to 1050 mm. The motors were designated M-105PF and M-105RF, respectively, and although the first powerplant was rushed into series production after testing, the second turned out to be less successful. The M-105PF, which was originally intended for fighter use and featured a less advantageous propeller gear ratio, was fitted to the Pe-2. This provided something of an increase in speed for the 'Peshka' at low level, but it fell away at altitude owing to a reduction in propeller efficiency.

Factory Nos 22 and 39 produced 2392 Pe-2s in 1942, and labour intensity was reduced to 13,200 man-hours compared with 25,300.

In the spring of 1943, Factory No 22 (with V M Myasishchev now filling the role of chief designer) was tasked with bringing about a marked improvement in the performance of the Pe-2. The principal external difference in machines of this improved type was that the pitot-static tube was moved to the windscreen on the pilot's cockpit. Apart from that, cowlings were fitted to the airbrake grids, and on some series aircraft individual engine exhaust pipes were fitted instead of manifolds. Series production aircraft No 19/205, with a takeoff weight of 8550 kg (18,845 lbs), developed a maximum speed of 521 km/h at an altitude of 3700 metres (323.5 mph at 12,140 ft) during testing in August 1943.

A further series of small changes were incorporated into the design of the Pe-2 in the first half of 1944. All aircraft were fitted with individual exhaust pipes, the radio, bombsight and oxygen equipment were changed, as was the cockpit instrumentation,

In the final Pe-2 configuration the navigator's open turret was replaced by a VUB-1 rotating turret mount fitted with a UBK 12.7 mm machine gun. The VUB-1 significantly improved firing angles and eased the navigator's working conditions by protecting his position from the elements. The lower hatch mount of the radio-operator/gunner was fitted with a UBT 12.7 mm machine gun, while the spherical side mounts in the fuselage had a ShKAS 7.62 mm machine gun that could be relocated from one side to the other as necessary

The UPe-2 trainer had an instructor's cabin mounted behind the student's cockpit. Such trainers were used extensively during 1944-45, when the requirements for the training of new pilots were upgraded

A series Pe-2 with powerful M-82F radial engines. Contrary to expectations, this variant was not extensively used owing to the insufficient reliability of the powerplant and its high fuel consumption, which limited range. In addition, a decision was made to install this engine in the Tu-2 bomber and reconnaissance aircraft

and small aerodynamic refinements were made. The last big change in Pe-2 production came at the very end of 1944, when the shape of the leading edge of the outer wing sections was changed. This gave an increase of 10-15 km/h (6-9 mph) in the Pe-2's range of flying speeds, which greatly improved the aircraft's handling characteristics on landing. The Pe-2's ceiling also increased by 600-800 metres (1970-2625 ft).

By December 1944, a series production Pe-2 boasted a normal takeoff weight of 8400 kg (18,520 lbs), and could achieve a low-level flying speed of 464 km/h (288 mph) and 524 km/h at 3900-4000 metres (325 mph at 12,800-13,100 ft). Its range at an altitude of 1000 metres (3300 ft) was 1100 km (680 miles) at exactly 80 per cent of maximum speed, and the dive-bomber's greatest range was 1300 km (800 miles).

PHOTO-RECONNAISSANCE

From the outset of the Great Patriotic War in June 1941, the Pe-2 was also the preferred candidate for the reconnaissance role, as it had a sufficiently high speed, could carry heavy photographic equipment, was well armed and had good survivability. The first long-range reconnaissance aircraft, fitted with AFA-1 cameras and underslung fuel tanks, were factory numbers 3/25 and 12/27, built as prototypes in July 1941. These were followed by four short-range reconnaissance aircraft that had been hastily reworked to perform this mission through the installation of four aerial cameras in the bomb-bay.

Parallel to the bombers, a reconnaissance variant designated 'Pe-2 reconnaissance' entered series production in August 1941 at Factory No 22. Subsequently the average monthly production for these aircraft would sometimes reach 15-20 examples a month – that is to say seven to ten per cent of the Pe-2s manufactured. There was no separate record kept of the number of Pe-2s built, but a rough estimate based on known production rates would put the overall figure at 700-800 aircraft.

Early series examples of the Pe-2 served as the basis for the reconnaissance variant, which meant that these machines lacked many of the characteristic

features seen in late-build 'Peshkas' such as differences in weaponry, aerodynamic improvements, more powerful engines and modified outer wing shape. The factory-produced reconnaissance aircraft (bombers in operational units were also being converted into reconnaissance aircraft on site) had no airbrake grids, and were finished more thoroughly.

The performance of these machines was slightly better than that of standard early series bombers.

As a rule reconnaissance aircraft had increased fuel reserves thanks to the use of underslung cigar-shaped jettisonable fuel tanks, which were made from kraft-cellulose greased with casein adhesive for pressurisation. It was possible to carry 290-300 litres (64-66 gallons) of fuel in tanks such as these, and although their external mounting reduced the aircraft's maximum speed by 30-35 km/h (18-22 mph), range increased by up to 625-650 km (390-400 miles).

Special equipment for reconnaissance aircraft differed somewhat from that fitted in Pe-2 bombers. The automatic dive control unit was removed, but an AK-1 automatic navigational control unit was installed. This stabilised the aircraft about the vertical axis by acting on the rudder. The AK-1 ensured that a heading could be maintained to an accuracy of 1-2 degrees, relieving the pilot of this responsibility. From the end of 1941 to early 1942, reconnaissance variants of the Pe-2 were the only examples fitted with fixed loop radio compasses.

The principal difference was in the provision of photographic apparatus. The first reconnaissance Pe-2s were fitted with two large vertical AFA-1 cameras in the bomb-bay. These had two types of lens with focusing distances of 30 cm and 50 cm (11.8 in and 19.7 in). When the AFA-1s were installed the standard bomb-bay doors were replaced by convex ones with cut-outs for the lenses. The navigator operated the AFA-1s, while a special NAFA-19 stills camera for night photography could be installed in the gunner's cockpit instead of the standard AFA-B equipment. The shutter was activated via a signal from the photocell after it had captured the glare of the photo-flash bomb.

From 1942 updated AFA-3S and AFA-33 cameras with a focusing distance of 100 cm (39.3 in) began to be used in operational units, along with American K-17s, which arrived via Lend-Lease. With the aim of increasing the area that could be surveyed in a single approach, operational units would sometimes resort to using dual cameras. Typically, new cameras would be used in conjunction with the original equipment, and by pivoting the latter double the area could be covered photographically.

There was also a variant of the Pe-3 nightfighter equipped for photographic reconnaissance (it was sometimes known as the Pe-3R or the Pe-3F). It has to be said that reconnaissance aviation crews expressed a preference for the Pe-3 over the Pe-2, as the former had greater range and was armed with a cannon. On this machine the cameras were not located in the bomb-bay (which was filled with an extra fuel tank), but in the aft section of the fuselage.

The Pe-3 heavy fighter was created by introducing minor changes into the Pe-2 design. It differed externally to the latter aircraft by having an additional large-calibre machine gun in the forward fuselage, the barrel of which protruded from the front lower glazing panel. The Pe-3 also lacked the hatch-mounted rear-facing ventral machine gun, and windows in the rear fuselage were covered over

GUARDS BOMBER AIR REGIMENTS

Guards formations (comprising four armoured divisions) first appeared in the Red Army line-up on 18 September 1941 in commemoration of the successful counterattack outside Yelnya, where for the first time so far in the Great Patriotic War German troops were beaten back from a comparatively large population centre with tens of thousands of inhabitants. This tradition of awarding combat units, both formations and amalgamations, the title of Guards units spread later to the VVS RKKA (*Voenno-Vozdushnye Sily Raboche-Krestyanskoy Krasnoy Armii* – Air Force of the Workers' and Peasants' Red Army) and Soviet Navy. As a rule it would follow a success in battle against the German invaders (and later against Japanese forces in Manchuria).

The seemingly relentless German advance on Moscow was stopped conclusively in early December 1941. Furthermore, on the 5th of the month forces on the Western Front, supported by aviation units, launched a counterattack that would eventually beat back German troops specifically targeting the capital of the USSR and scatter them up to 200-300 miles in various directions. On 6 December, in an effort to further boost the fighting spirit of aviation units defending the Soviet capital, the People's Commissar of Defence decreed that six VVS RKKA units which had distinguished themselves in the defence of Moscow and Leningrad were to be awarded the Guards title. This order was announced just hours after the counterattack had commenced.

4th GvBAP

The first Guards Air Regiment to be equipped with the Pe-2 was 4th GvBAP (*Gvardveyskiy Bombardirovochniy Aviapolk* – Guards Bomber Air Regiment). This unit had originally been formed on 17 April 1938 at Smolensk airfield as 31st SBAP (*Skorostnoy Bombardirovochniy Aviapolk* – Fast Bomber Air Regiment), consisting of five squadrons. The regiment was initially led by Col V E Nestertsev, who would later become the commander of the Air Corps of Long Range Aviation.

31st SBAP was equipped with the Polikarpov R-5 and Tupolev R-6 reconnaissance aircraft, but assimilation with the advanced, high-speed, twin-engined SB bomber started within a month of the regiment's formation. The first three squadrons to convert participated in a flypast over Smolensk on 7 November.

Nestertsev was promoted at the beginning of December, and Capt F I Dobysh was named commander of the unit. Its conversion to the SB was completed by the spring of 1939 under his leadership. Later that year the regiment saw action during the Russo-Finnish Winter War, which commenced in late November, as part of 16th BAB (*Bombardirovochnaya Aviatsionnaya Brigada* – Bomber Air Brigade). Crews flew some 1000 sorties in just over three months, and during the course of these missions 23 aviators were killed and 32 were injured.

A total of 230 servicemen from 31st SBAP were awarded orders and medals for their distinguished service in carrying out military objectives during this conflict. On 7 April 1940 four of them were awarded the title of Hero of the Soviet Union – Capt Konstantin Orlov (posthumously, as his aircraft had exploded in mid-air during his 19th sortie), Lts Nikolai Stolnikov and Ivan Khudyakov and MSgt Grigoriy Guslev. The latter three were all members of one crew. Their SB was shot down and made an emergency landing on a frozen lake. They had all been wounded prior to force-landing on the ice, and their capture seemed likely until two R-5s landed close by and collected the injured aviators.

Following a year of peacetime flying at Smolensk after the cessation of hostilities with Finland, the regiment received orders in May 1941 from Air Force Command for the special Baltic military district that saw three squadrons from 31st SBAP move to the forward airfield at Mitava (Elgava) and two more head to Platon.

On the evening of 21 June 1941, unit commander Fedor Dobysh issued orders to disperse all SBs around the operational aprons at Mitava and Platon. As a result not one of the regiment's aircraft was destroyed on the ground during Luftwaffe bombing raids the following morning.

At 1130 hrs that same day, Dobysh personally led a group of 50 SBs on a sortie to strike the advancing enemy forces. Considerable damage was inflicted on German motorised columns as a result of the bombing, and not one aircraft was lost. Alas, the next sortie (a strike against enemy tanks at Kalvara) was less successful, with four crews failing to return. Those that survived reported that four Bf 109s had been destroyed by the gunners' defensive fire.

Two group sorties on 24 June ended with contrasting results for 31st SBAP. The first strike, consisting of 40 bombers, saw crews successfully strike targets in East Prussia without loss. However, eight SBs led aloft by Snr Lt Sarkis Ayrapetov several hours after this raid were lost without trace. It later became apparent that only six men had survived from the downed SBs, the remaining 18 crewmen, including the squadron leader, having been killed. One of those to die was Senior Political Instructor Sarkis Ayrapetov, who steered his burning aircraft towards a concentration of enemy weaponry in one of the war's first fire-ram attacks.

In the terrible battles of late June and early July 1941 the regiment lost almost all of its aircraft. Indeed, by 15 July, when the remnants of 31st SBAP were redeployed to Monino, in the Moscow Region, only seven SBs survived from the 59 originally on strength less than a month earlier. Around a quarter of 31st SBAP crews – 49 pilots, navigators and gunners – had either been killed or were missing without trace. By the time the regiment was re-formed in August and issued with Pe-2s, the number of squadrons it controlled had been reduced, first to three (led by Capts Morozov, Tupol and Zorin) and then two.

These units were manned by recent flying school graduates who had completed their training ahead of time in order to fill the posts of rank-and-file pilots. Conversion to a new aircraft that was quite difficult to fly did not come easily to them, especially when it came to landings.

Experienced pilots, however, were quick to appreciate the Pe-2's improved survivability over the SB, as well as its more powerful weaponry and higher maximum speed. By the onset of autumn the regiment had 20 new 'Peshkas' at its disposal, and 14 crews were passed out as combat ready.

On 9 September 31st SBAP left Monino for the Karelian Region (whose airfields were at Shug-ozero and Derevyannaya) under the command of the Air Forces of 7th Separate Army. From 15 September to 14 October the unit flew 325 sorties, destroying five crossing points, four trains and up to 50 vehicles. The fighting became particularly intense when Finnish forces reached the Svir River and cut off the Kirov railway line.

On 16 October the Germans began to attack Tikhvin, and when the Finns and the Germans met east of Ladoga it appeared that Leningrad was surrounded on all sides. The principal forces of the VVS RKKA's 7th Army Air Force were duly redirected towards the besieged town of Tikhvin. From 10 November to 13 December, aircraft from the 7th Army Air Force flew 692 sorties (including 85 by Pe-2s) in an attempt to break down concentrations of enemy forces. The most experienced crews took to the skies several times a day in support of the Red Army, often battling unfavourable meteorological conditions – light drizzle and fog – while taking the fight to the enemy.

On one such mission, on 15 November, a group of Pe-2s targeted German artillery batteries around Tikhvin. On the second approach to the target a shell hit Lt Boris Afonin's aircraft, knocking out its port engine. The crew commander tried to hold the Pe-2 in level flight, but shrapnel from a second round destroyed the tailplane support and vibration set in. With the help of his navigator, Afonin flew the crippled Petlyakov away from the target area, but suffered a catastrophic loss of altitude in the process.

As they headed back towards Soviet lines, their flight path took them over a dense forest. Spotting a clearing ahead, Afonin reacted instantly, turning the aircraft towards it. Moments later there was a crash, a deafening noise and clouds of snow dust. Afonin, who was the first to regain consciousness, helped to free his navigator, Ivan Karpov, who was trapped in the cockpit. After reporting the location of Afonin's aircraft, the regiment commander (who was circling above in a Pe-2) rapidly organised a rescue team, which that same day retrieved the injured crew and took them to a nearby hospital.

As previously noted, in an order from the People's Commissariat for Defence, dated 6 December 1941, 31st BAP became the first VVS RKKA bomber regiment to be transformed into a Guards regiment. It received the designation 4th GvBAP for 'courage demonstrated during air combat with the German fascist invaders, and for the steadfastness, fortitude and heroism of its crews'. Aside from 31st SBAP, Guards titling was also bestowed upon four fighter and one ground attack regiment at this time.

Lt Col Fedor Dobysh's crew in front of a Pe-2 that boasts crocodile nose art. Dobysh, who was then CO of 4th GvBAP, is in the centre

The change of designation to 4th GvBAP signalled the regiment's transformation into a three-squadron format, as well as a one-and-a-half fold increase in the officers' financial allowance and a two-fold increase for sergeants and rank-and-file personnel. As a rule the Guards units were also better equipped in terms of aircraft and aircrew. Thus, on 9 April 1942, 4th GvBAP had 32 Pe-2s at its disposal. This proved to be the regiment's peak strength, however, as the heavy and, for the Red Army, unsuccessful battles of the autumn and winter of 1942 on the southern sector of the Soviet-German Front, and the considerable stabilisation of the situation around Leningrad, led to further reinforcements being halted. Moreover, many experienced commanders were promoted and left for other posts, including Guards Col Dobysh, who became the commander of 263rd BAP in June 1942. His place was taken by Guards Lt Col Perepelitsa.

In September of that year 4th GvBAP was reassigned to 14th Air Army on the Volkhov Front, where it would fight as part of 280th BAD (*Bombardirovochniy Aviatsionniy Diviziya* – Bomber Aviation Division) under Lt Col N N Buyanskiy.

After the siege of Leningrad had been temporarily broken in early January 1943, between the 12th and 15th of the month the regiment was called upon to strike the forward edge of the enemy's defences. The bombers were effective against assets in the rear, and they also disrupted enemy communications. As a result of just one raid by six Pe-2s on the railway station at Mga on 14 January, six wagons, together with station structures, were destroyed by direct hits.

By the beginning of February 1943 there were just 15 Pe-2s and four ageing SBs on strength with 4th GvBAP. At about this time crews from the unit recorded their first encounters with Luftwaffe Fw 190A fighters, and their powerful weaponry. Three Pe-2s were lost to attacks by Focke-Wulfs in a month, including the aircraft of squadron commander Guards Maj Trubytsin, and a further two 'Peshkas' were damaged. One Fw 190A was reportedly shot down by defensive fire.

The official history of 4th GvBAP records that, as of the end of April 1943, the regiment had destroyed more than 250 tanks and 400 vehicles, 14 trains, 20 warehouses and two fuel dumps set on fire and destroyed, four transport vessels sunk or damaged and 41 enemy aircraft were left burnt out on the ground. Pe-2 crews had also been credited with downing 38 enemy aircraft.

Maj Pavel Semak, a squadron commander in 4th GvBAP, receives the Star of the Hero of the Soviet Union from Mikhail Kalinin, Chairman of the Presidium of the Supreme Soviet

At the beginning of 1944 4th GvBAP took part in the operation to permanently break the siege of Leningrad. On 20 January the regiment was awarded the honourable title of 'Novgorod' following successful attacks on German troops during the course of the Leningrad offensive. 4th GvBAP would subsequently fight as part of 13th Air Army on the Leningrad Front and, from July 1944, as part of 14th Air Army, which was already on the Third Baltic Front.

From early October 1944 Soviet aerial reconnaissance detected a build-up of various enemy ships, vehicle transporters and combat equipment in the Latvian port of Ainazi. The retreating Germans planned to cross to the other side of the Gulf of Riga by sea, as all the roads leading to the Latvian capital south of Ainazi had already been closed. Squadrons from 4th GvBAP, led by Guards Capt P S Semak, struck the vessels and the nearby loading pier. Their attack prevented hundreds of German soldiers from crossing the gulf and strengthening the defence of Riga. On 13 October 1944 the city was liberated by Soviet troops, and later that same day those forces were congratulated on their success by the Soviet High Command.

In the final months of the war in Europe 4th GvBAP saw action against a large concentration of enemy forces (500,000+ troops) cut off in Latvia. Defending an area known as 'Fortress Kurland', the German and Latvian troops repelled attack after attack by the Red Army, whose troops were supported by 4th GvBAP in their endeavours through to war's end.

8th GvBAP

Formed in 1938 as 5th SBAP, which was in turn part of 15th BAB, this regiment initially operated four-engined Tupolev TB-3s from Kirovograd. By June 1939 the unit had re-equipped with twin-engined SBs. On 26 February 1940 the regiment sent 40 SBs (under the command of Maj F P Kotlyar) to the northern airfield of Sula-Yarvi, where they became part of 7th Army Air Force. Immediately committed to combat against Finnish forces, 5th SBAP crews flew 402 sorties in less than 20 days, destroying dams and bombing the port town of Vyborg and the railway station at Vipuri. Just four SBs and three crews were lost during this period of intense action.

The German invasion of the USSR in June 1941 found 5th SBAP based at Kulincha airfield, not far from Odessa. On 22 June the regiment, which was part of 21st SAD (*Smeshannaya Aviatsionnaya Diviziya* – Combined Aviation Division), had 31 SBs and 25 Pe-2s at its disposal – the unit was only halfway through its conversion to the 'Peshka' at this time. By dawn on the 22nd the aviation units in the Odessa military district had been dispersed around the operational airfields, thereby avoiding losses on the ground. The following morning, however, a surprise enemy attack on Kulincha destroyed five Pe-2s belonging to 5th SBAP.

From the very beginning of the war, crews from the regiment carried out bombing raids on advancing Rumanian and German forces. Aside from tactical targets such as the enemy's mechanised units, supply convoys and floating crossings, 5th SBAP crews bombed Brailov and Galati airfields, participated in raids on the oil refineries in Ploesti and destroyed large railway junctions and bridges. Amongst the latter targets was the Galati bridge, which was attacked by two groups of nine bombers on 22 June 1941.

By the end of June the combat strength for 5th SBAP remained at 24 SBs and 20 Pe-2s, despite ten days of near-constant action. These numbers took a hit on 4 July, however, in what turned out to be one of the blackest days for the regiment. Two 'Peshkas' and five SBs failed to return to base, their loss leading to the decision that in future the regiment would operate as much as possible at night or in twilight.

A line-up of 8th GvBAP personnel during the regiment's investiture with the Guards Banner in March 1942. The unit was commanded by Lt Col F P Kotlyar from October 1938 to February 1942, when he was replaced by Maj G S Kucherkov, who accepted the banner at the investiture

The commander of the second squadron, Capt Viktor Vasilyevich Anisimov, was named as one of the most courageous pilots in 5th SBAP during this period, having led groups of bombers to their targets on more than 15 occasions in the course of the first month of fighting. On 30 July Anisimov and his crew perished when their bomber was shot down by German anti-aircraft fire close to the Ukrainian city of Uman. In Anisimov's posthumous recommendation for the title of Hero of the Soviet Union it was indicated that the courageous pilot had crashed his Pe-2 into a 'concentration of German technology'. Although this was no premeditated fire-ram attack, it has to be noted that Anisimov fully deserved the distinguished title of Hero of the Soviet. And it was the bombs dropped by his crew that ruined the Galati bridge.

On 2 August 1941 German tanks broke through to Shaytarovka, where 5th SBAP's Pe-2s were now based. Taken by surprise, the regiment was forced to abandon its aircraft as virtually defenceless personnel fled for their lives in the face of enemy Panzers. The regiment suffered its greatest losses of the entire war on that day, yet it resumed military action just a week later. As of 26 August 5th SBAP possessed just five serviceable and five unserviceable Pe-2s. The SBs (nine in total), which had been spared the Panzer attack of 2 August, were handed over to 5th SBAP's dedicated night attack squadron. This unit was led by Maj F P Kotlyar, who had conceded leadership of the 'day' regiment, now equipped exclusively with 'Peshkas', to Col G S Kucherkov.

In total, losses for 5th SBAP to all causes were 32 Pe-2s and 20 SBs in two months of fighting.

Up until March 1942, when the regiment was designated 8th GvBAP, it was under 21st SAD control. The unit was then briefly incorporated into 5th RAG (*Reservnaya Aviatsionnaya Gruppa* – Reserve Aviation Group), and on 5 May 1942 it became part of 219th BAD, which fought as part of the Air Forces of the Southern Front.

In 13 months of fighting with the Pe-2 and SB the regiment had flown 3166 sorties and amassed 4132 flying hours, including 365 hours of night flying. On 27 July 1942 8th GvBAP, under the command of Guards Lt Col G S Kucherkov, handed over its remaining aircraft to other units in 219th BAD and left for Kirovobad to convert to the Douglas Boston III and A-20B. This process proved to be a lengthy one, and the regiment finally reappeared at the front in July 1943 just in time to participate in the pivotal battle for the Kursk Salient as part of 221st BAD. 8th GvBAP continued to fly the American-built Douglas 'bombing twin' through to VE Day.

10th GvBAP

On 7 March 1942, at the same time as 8th GvBAP was created, a second bomber regiment was formed and designated 10th GvBAP. It had previously been known as 33rd SBAP of 19th SAD, part of the Air Forces of the South Western Front. This unit had also gained combat experience by the start of the Great Patriotic War, having sent two of its SB-equipped units to Mongolia to counter Japanese aggression along the Khalkhin Gol River in the summer of 1939. In January of the following year the entire regiment was transferred to the Kola Peninsula, where it participated in the Winter War with Finland, flying 318 sorties.

On 22 June 1941 33rd SBAP, led by Lt Col F S Pushkarevych, was incorporated into the Air Forces of the Kiev special military district, being based at Belaya Tserkov with 24 SBs, 22 Arkhangelskii Ar-2s (heavily modified and re-engined SBs) and 14 Pe-2s, although crews for the latter aircraft were not yet fully trained on the type.

From the very beginning of the fighting the regiment was bombing mechanised enemy columns in the direction of Brody, Sokal and Zhitomyr, operating from an altitude of 400-700 metres (1200-3300 ft) without fighter cover. By 1 July 33rd SBAP's combat strength had been reduced to 24 SB and Ar-2 bombers and nine Pe-2s. Despite an ever-dwindling number of aircraft, crews from the regiment had flown up to 70 combat sorties a day during this period. They twice received the grateful thanks of the head of the Air Forces of the South Western Front, Gen F A Astakhov – on 10 July for a successful attack on an advancing enemy tank unit, and on 25 August for the destruction of a bridge across the River Dnepr near Okuninovo. In the latter operation V S Yefremov's crew distinguished themselves. Yefremov would subsequently be awarded the title of Hero of the Soviet Union on two separate occasions.

In August 1941 the number of squadrons in the regiment was reduced to three, and then just two in December. Maj K I Rasskazov was made commander of 33rd SBAP in December 1941, the former squadron leader having been awarded the Order of Lenin on 6 November.

From 22 June 1941 through to 7 March 1942, the unit flew 1519 combat sorties (410 of these at night). In total its crews dropped 792 tonnes (779 tons) of bombs and more than 5000 ampoules on the enemy,

A group of 8th GvBAP personnel sing the national anthem shortly after being presented with the Guards Banner. The unit was equipped with early-series Pe-2s at this time, the aircraft featuring only a small amount of nose glazing. The star insignia worn by the bombers lacked a white outline at this early stage in the war, and the Pe-2s had no tactical numbers on the fuselage or vertical tail surfaces

the latter containing the inflammable liquid 'KS'. These weapons were dubbed 'Molotov cocktails' in the West. According to reports from crews, 19 enemy aircraft were destroyed in aerial combat and a further 22 set ablaze on their airfields. The Germans had also lost up to 450 vehicles and six trains as a result of attacks by 33rd SBAP.

Only two Ar-2s, a single Pe-2 and 11 SBs remained on the regiment's strength by 1 March 1942. Six days later the unit became 10th GvBAP, whereupon it was retrained as a night bombing regiment. Fighting as part of the Air Forces of the South Western Front, the regiment soon found that the 'Peshka' was poorly suited to night operations, having a high landing speed that placed considerable demands on the pilot's flying technique. Consequently, the regiment predominantly flew the SB (as well as a small number of Ilyushin DB-3s from mid-1942), but from April 1943 it was equipped with Douglas A-20B/Gs.

The unit came under the control of 6th GvBAD (*Gvardeyskaya Bombardirovochnaya Aviadiviziya* – Guards Bomber Air Division) in December 1943, the division being made up of three regiments in total – the remaining two flew Pe-2s exclusively. In February-March 1945 the personnel of 10th GvBAP were sent to the rear to convert to the new Tupolev Tu-2 bomber, but the unit was then transferred to Mongolia in early August in order to take the fight to Japan. In the early hours of 9 August 10th GvBAP carried out bombing raids on Japanese troops in Manchuria. Within a few weeks the war with the Imperial Kwantung Army was over, however.

This period 'combat history' of 8th GvBAP shows how the unit moved through Stalingrad, the Kursk Salient, northern Ukraine and Poland, before ending up in Berlin

34th GvBAP

The 34th GvBAP was initially formed as the 44th SBAP in the late 1930s. It was the first VVS RKKA bomber unit to see action in the Red Army's 'freedom march into the eastern regions of Poland' in September 1939, and it also played an active role in the Winter War with Finland. The regiment fought as part of 55th BAB, which came under the Air Forces of the 7th Army, and was awarded the order of the Red Banner for its successes in combat. On 1 May 1941 six groups of nine SBs from 44th SBAP took part in the May Day Parade in Moscow.

Upon the outbreak of the Great Patriotic War 44th SBAP served under 2nd SAD of the Air Forces of the Leningrad special military district, flying from Tulembel airfield, near Staraya Russa. On 24 June the regiment had 39 SBs and one Pe-2 on strength, the latter aircraft having been issued to the unit for general training and continuous flight and groundcrew assimilation.

On 24 August 44th SBAP, which had been transferred to the Air Forces of the Leningrad Front (along with 2nd SAD), had just eight serviceable and two unserviceable SBs left. By then the regiment was based at Shugozero airfield, near Tikhvin, and it carried out raids on German forces that were attempting to surround Leningrad.

In September-October 1941 the remnants of 44th SBAP were sent to the rear to regroup. Crews duly converted to the Pe-2 dive-bomber, but because there was a lack of new aircraft available the regiment was reduced in strength to two squadrons of SBs and trained in night flying. This meant that losses were appreciably reduced and bombing raids remained sufficiently effective, despite 44th having to make do with the obsolete SB. Flying more than 300 combat sorties in November-December 1941, the regiment specifically targeted German forces around Tikhvin.

During the early summer of 1942 Pe-2 dive-bombers began to reach the regiment in modest numbers. These aircraft were flown predominantly during the day, leaving the night work to the SBs. On 12 July 1942 the Pe-2 of flight commander Capt S M Aleshin was shot down during a raid on the railway station at Lemblovo. Having served with 44th SBAP from 1941 (he had completed 117 combat sorties, 88 of them at night), Aleshin preferred a heroic death over capture. According to the testimony of the other participants in the raid on Lemblovo, his 'Peshka' was capable of being steered right up to the last moment, when it crashed into an enemy artillery battery. Navigator Lt V A Goncharuk and radio-operator/gunner SSgt N A Borbov died alongside the commander. All three members of the crew were posthumously awarded the title of Hero of the Soviet Union via a decree from the Presidium of the Supreme Soviet of the USSR, dated 10 February 1943.

Having become 34th GvBAP on 22 November 1942, the regiment became part of 276th BAD of 13th Air Army on the Leningrad Front later that same month. As of 1 December 1942 there were only two aircraft listed on its strength, yet by the start of Operation *Iskra* (the offensive aimed at breaking the siege of Leningrad) on 12 January 1943, the unit had been augmented up to full three-squadron strength in terms of crews and materiel.

13 April 1943 turned out to be a black day for 34th GvBAP. A group of six aircraft under the command of squadron leader Guards Maj I F Kovanev took off on a sortie, escorted by eight Yak-7 fighters. The target – the airfield at Krasnogvardeysk – would be a wasps' nest of enemy fighters. The group was attacked by German flak batteries en route to the target, wounding a navigator and radio-operator/gunner. The Soviet fighters lost the bombers while manoeuvring in cloud in an attempt to avoid flak. Fw 190s then appeared and shot down the aeroplanes of Guards Capt Golovanov and Guards Lt Golikov. The four remaining Pe-2s in the formation, having broken away from the constant attacks by fighters, bombed the aircraft on the apron at Krasnogvardeysk airfield.

On the return journey the group was attacked by enemy fighters close to Taytsa, as a result of which the Pe-2 of Guards Jnr Lt Polkovnikov caught fire, broke up in mid-air at an altitude of 500-600 metres (1600-1900 ft) and crashed in enemy territory. The navigator and radio-operator/gunner of Guards Maj Kovanev's crew were also wounded during this attack. On their approach to Pulkovo the three remaining Pe-2s in the formation were once again attacked by enemy fighters, the 'Peshkas' on both sides of the formation being set ablaze. Only Guards Maj Kovanev managed to nurse his Pe-2 back to base, where more than 50 holes were found in the aircraft.

On 4 May 1943 34th GvBAP was awarded the honourable title of 'Tikhvin' for its active role in the operation to defend the town. On 9 July 1943 the regiment carried out a successful bombing raid on the German fighter airfield at Siverskaya, where the aircraft involved in 34th GvBAP's disastrous mission of 13 April were probably based. Sixteen days later six Pe-2s destroyed the vital bridge across the River Mga with two direct hits. This crossing had been actively used by the Germans to re-supply troops in the frontline.

On 28 August eight 'Peshkas' dive-bombed echelons of troops boarding trains at Tosno railway station, setting three trains ablaze.

In early 1944 34th GvBAP took part in the operation to bring the siege of Leningrad to an end. As part of this campaign, on 26 February nine Pe-2s, guided to the target by squadron navigator Capt V M Domnikov, carried out a raid on the airfield at Tartu. Aerial reconnaissance the following day established that 24 enemy aircraft had been set on fire. In June 1944 the regiment participated in the Vyborg operation on the Karelian Isthmus, which was aimed at breaking through the powerful Mannerheim Line. The latter consisted of long-standing defensive structures, while German and Finnish troops manning the line had vast stockpiles of ordnance. It was up to Pe-2 units such as 34th GvBAP to weaken the defences and reduce ordnance stockpiles through precision dive-bombing attacks.

This late-war Pe-2 of 34th GvBAP features nose art that consists of a white bear motif

In July the regiment, as part of 13th Air Army, supported advancing troops on the Leningrad Front during the Narva and, in September, the Tallinn offensives. From 15 October through to war's end, 34th GvBAP fought on the Third Belarusian Front as part of 1st Air Army, supporting the activities of frontline troops as they occupied East Prussia.

35th GvBAP

Formed as 150th SBAP and led by Maj I S Polbin, this regiment was based in the Zabaykal region of southeastern USSR, near the city of Chita, until the beginning of the Great Patriotic War. Just six days prior to the German invasion of the Soviet Union, 150th SBAP received an order to redeploy east to the VVS RKKA's European sector. Its SBs were dismantled and transported on railway wagons, the regiment eventually arriving in Rzhev during the first week of July 1941. Here, it was split into a three-squadron SBAP (High-Speed Bomber Air Regiment) led by Polbin and a two-squadron BBAP (Short Range Bomber Air Regiment) led by Maj Klobukov that would subsequently become a Ground Attack Air Regiment.

The first sortie for the bombers of 150th SBAP was made on 16 July, and was completed without loss to the regiment. Soon, however, two SBs were lost as a result of encounters with German 'Messerschmitts' and enemy artillery fire, the regimental commander's aircraft being one of the aircraft shot down. 150th SBAP would fly up to six combat sorties a day, returning to Rzhev airfield in twilight or sometimes in complete darkness. On 28 July one of the regiment's crews discovered, and successfully bombed, a large enemy communications centre in difficult weather conditions. This success was marked by the first combat awards given to aviators from 150th SBAP during the Great Patriotic War.

Polbin's pilots, and their successes in combat, were not only noticed by the commanders of Air Forces on the South Western Front. The newspaper *Stalin's Swift* featured a lengthy article in which it was stated, 'In five days commander Polbin's pilots have destroyed 17 enemy aircraft, two tanks, 64 vehicles carrying infantry or cargoes and 27 wagons carrying ammunition'. The regimental commander continued to personally lead groups of aircraft to their targets during daylight missions, but at night he would fly with one of his best pilots, future Hero of the Soviet Union Capt V G Ushakov.

Up until the end of 1941 crews from 150th SBAP had flown 2404 combat sorties, of which 753 had been made at night. According to reports from pilots and navigators, 27 enemy aircraft had been set on fire on the ground, as well as more than 650 vehicles, 250 tanks and around 170 railway wagons. The price paid by the unit for this success was high, however, as it lost 49 SBs and had 35 pilots, 30 navigators and 29 radio-operator/gunners killed.

In early February 1942 the regiment relinquished its surviving aircraft and was sent to the rear to regroup. It was brought up to strength with newly trained personnel who then completed their conversion to the Pe-2. This process took until the beginning of May to complete. The regiment continued to be led by I S Polbin, who had been promoted to the rank of lieutenant colonel. His successful leadership of the unit in 1941 had brought his name 'to the attention' of the upper Soviet leadership, and 150th SBAP was rewarded by being transferred to a special aviation group commanded by the son of Joseph Stalin, Col V I Stalin.

Within this group, 150th SBAP was tasked with flying night intruder missions on the Stalingrad Front. The unit also included a crack fighter regiment in the form of 434th IAP (*Istrebitel'nyy Aviatsionniy Polk* – Fighter Aviation Regiment) under Maj I I Kleshchev. The command hoped that the well-trained crews of this special group would set an example for demoralised VVS RKKA units that had suffered so badly during the recent fighting over Stalingrad.

150th SBAP certainly enhanced its reputation during 1942, with Lt Col I S Polbin and Capt Zholudev performing its most widely reported exploit when, in a surprise dive-bombing attack close to the village of Morozovsk, they destroyed a large fuel store that had allowed Bf 109s to operate from forward airfields. Railway yards and mechanised enemy columns were also routinely targeted by Polbin's regiment.

Yet despite these successes, the enemy forces ranged against the VVS RKKA on the southern sector of the Soviet-German Front were just too great. The Luftwaffe had deliberately focused the bulk of its units in this area of the vast frontline, thus allowing fighter units to gain air superiority. As a result both Kleshchev's and Polbin's regiments suffered heavy losses in July-August 1942. For example, during a raid on the German airfield at Millerovo 150th SBAP lost no fewer than seven of the 15 Pe-2s that had been sent aloft – two Heroes of the Soviet Union and their crews were among those who did not return. This time the active phase of the 150th SBAP's presence at the front did not exceed one month. From 13 July to 2 August the regiment, having carried out 406 combat sorties, 70 of which were at night, lost 12 Pe-2s and 24 aircrew.

The contribution of Polbin's regiment to Red Army success at Stalingrad was considered to be impressive by the VVS RKKA. Indeed, I S Polbin was recommended for the title of Hero of the Soviet Union, having flown 107 combat sorties (74 at night) up to the beginning of August 1942. He was also promoted to the rank of full colonel and transferred to the Red Army Air Force Inspectorate. Maj V A Novikov became the regiment's new commander, and 150th SBAP was re-formed as 35th GvBAP under the control of 285th BAD, led by Lt Col V A Sandalov. In 1943 it re-formed once again as 5th GvBAP, this time subordinate to 1st GvBAK (*Gvardeyskiy Bombardirovochniy Aviakorpus* – Guards Bomber Air Corps).

36th GvBAP

514th BAP was formed during the Great Patriotic War in September 1941, but it was by no means manned by complete novices, as the

Five distinguished pilots of 150th SBAP (the future 35th GvBAP), each of whom was awarded three Orders of the Red Banner. Regiment commander Lt Col Ivan Polbin is in the centre of the photograph, and to his left is the regiment's first Hero of the Soviet Union, Lt Fedor Demchenkov. During the summer of 1942 he became only the 61st Soviet soldier to be awarded this title in World War 2

regiment was given one squadron from 130th BAP and two from 125th BAP. The unit was equipped with 22 brand new Pe-2s and sent to the Northwestern Front under the command of Maj P S Lozenko, where it came under 6th SAD control.

In October 1941 a local offensive operation was carried out on the Northwestern Front in the area between the Ilmen and Seliger lakes. The only bomber regiment supporting the ground troops on this front was 514th BAP. In four months, crews from this unit flew more than 600 combat sorties and dropped 314 tonnes (309 tons) of bombs. Losses were relatively small – eight Pe-2s – while the 'Peshka' gunners and navigators claimed nine enemy aircraft destroyed.

In February 1942 the operation at Staraya Russa began, during which six German divisions were surrounded in the area around Demyansk and Staraya Russa. The Luftwaffe sent additional fighter units to the Northwestern Front to provide cover for transport aircraft and to protect the encircled concentrations of troops from Soviet bombers. Their arrival made combat operations for 514th BAP much more complicated. In less than a month nine Pe-2s were lost, along with their crews.

One of those to die at this time was Snr Lt I V Struzhkin, who had flown 123 combat sorties between 1 October 1941 and 25 February 1942. This remarkable pilot had participated in the combat testing of a retractable ski-equipped Pe-2 dive-bomber in the winter of 1941-42. And it was Struzhkin alone who knew how to find and photograph an enemy airfield that was accepting transport aircraft inside the Demyansk pocket. In February 1942 Snr Lt Struzhkin was recommended for the title of Hero of the Soviet Union, but he did not live to receive his award. On 6 April 1942 Struzhkin's aircraft was attacked by three Bf 109s over Lychkova, in the Novgorod region. His crew shot down one enemy aircraft, but the 'Peshka' was also damaged. Struzhkin ordered his crew to abandon the aircraft and was the last to bail out, but he was remorselessly shot by a German fighter pilot while he was descending in his parachute.

On 21 July 1942 four pilots and navigators of 514th BAP were made Heroes of the Soviet Union, and during the course of the war the highest award in the USSR was conferred on 12 of the regiment's aviators. Withdrawn to the rear to regroup in July, the regiment became 36th GvBAP on 22 November 1942.

Having completed a mission over the Kalinin Front in early 1942, this anonymous Pe-2 is pushed back into a dispersal site under the crowns of snow-covered fir trees so as to hide it from enemy aerial reconnaissance aircraft

From April 1943 the regiment came under the control of 202nd BAD (led by Col S I Nechiporenko), whose units were exclusively equipped with Pe-2 dive-bombers – the other regiments were 18th and 797th BAPs. From December 1943 this division fought as part of 4th BAK (*Bombardirovochniy Aviakorpus* – Bomber Air Corps) reserve of the Supreme High Command in the most intense sectors of the Soviet-German Front, ending the war in the skies over the German capital. 36th GvBAP's performance during the final weeks of the war in Europe earned it the honorary title 'Berlin'.

96th GvBAP

At the beginning of the war SB bomber-equipped 99th SBAP, under Lt Col S A Yegorov, was among the youngest of the Red Army regiments, having only been formed in May 1941. It was brought up to strength by flying-school and college graduates who had amassed the necessary flying experience during the snowy winter of 1940-41. The regiment's complement of aircraft was completed literally a few days before the outbreak of war.

On 26 June 1941 99th SBAP, having been redeployed to Priyamino airfield in Byelorussia, began to see military action in the vicinity of Minsk. Its principal targets during this period were the German crossing points over the River Berezina in the area around Bobruysk, and also columns of tanks and armoured vehicles around Smolevichi, Borisov, Minsk and Slutsk. The SB bombers flew in tight formations of nine aircraft at medium altitude without fighter cover when attacking these targets. Unsurprisingly, on 28 June, while attacking columns of tanks and the enemy airfield at Gorki, 23rd SAD (to which 99th SBAP was assigned) lost 17 aircraft of the 68 bound for the target, and the following day it lost 14 of the 55 that took off.

In less than a week 99th SBAP lost 35 of its 43 crews and, having handed over its surviving aircraft to other regiments in the division, withdrew to the rear to regroup. An aviation centre had by then evolved at Lipetsk, and it was here that the regiment converted to the Pe-2 bomber, being equipped with a force of 22 aircraft.

At the end of August 99th SBAP came under the control of 1st RAG (as the aviation formations temporarily assigned to frontline air forces were known in the initial period of the war), which was active on the Bryansk Front. Aside from the regiment, the reserve group had a ground attack and two fighter air regiments also on hand. With the

The crew of pilot Timofey Punev (second from left) of 36th GvBAP. Note the aircraft's nose art, which consists of the Guards insignia applied directly over the inscription *Vislenskiy*, the regiment's honorary name. The Pe-2 is clearly having maintenance performed on its engines

Red Army struggling to contain German forces at the front, the group was immediately thrown into action without having been briefed on the enemy's defensive strengths in the area. 1st RAG duly lost nine aircraft (including seven of 99th SBAP's Pe-2s) during the course of 125 combat sorties on its very first day of fighting.

In September 99th SBAP was transferred to 4th RAG, which was fighting on the Southwestern Front. Some of the sorties flown by the regiment during this period turned out to be very unusual. For example, Lt A P Smirnov was tasked with establishing contact with the commanders of 37th Army, which had been surrounded in the area around the airfield at Borispol, outside Kiev. The crews encountered a whirlwind of flak on their way to the target, one round making a large hole in one of the engines, while another damaged a propeller blade. Smirnov landed safely at Borispol, and along with other aviators he managed to repair the damage to his Pe-2 overnight. He then flew back, taking seven fighter pilots with him, crammed into the 'Peshka's' cramped cockpit.

In early June 1942 Maj A Ya Yakobson took command of 99th SBAP, while Lt Col S A Yegorov led 270th BAD, which directly controlled the regiment. Operationally, the summer of 1942 turned out to be no easier for the regiment than the previous summer had been. From early June to 20 August 99th SBAP had flown 143 missions, fighting on the Southwestern and Stalingrad Fronts. On 23 August, after handing its surviving 'Peshkas' over to other units, 99th SBAP was sent to Kazan to regroup. The training of new pilots and the formation of the regiment were completed on 2 November. Three days later Capt A P Smirnov (207 sorties by September 1942) and Snr Lt B S Bystriy became Heroes of the Soviet Union.

During the course of the Red Army's winter offensive of 1942-43, 99th SBAP operated from airfields at Dankov, Voronets and Yelets. On 1 May 1943 two new heroes joined the regiment, which had by then been designated 'Stalingrad' – squadron navigators Capts A P Krupin and A M Turikov. The latter flew with Hero of the Soviet Union A P Smirnov, and their radio-operator/air gunner Jnr Lt N B Stratiyevskiy was also subsequently awarded this title. Thus, this unique crew was comprised entirely of Heroes of the Soviet Union.

Capt A M Turikov was engaged in 75 air battles with enemy fighters, and he was shot down twice by anti-aircraft artillery and three times by fighters. He also sustained burns on three occasions while flying his aircraft. By February 1943 he had completed 145 combat sorties, flying 204 in total. Forty of these were reconnaissance missions far beyond enemy lines. Turikov was group leader for 150 sorties, and he was engaged in 170 dogfights with enemy fighters – he personally destroyed six aircraft using large-calibre machine guns.

On 16 July 1943 99th SBAP became 96th GvBAP. It was the first regiment both in its division and in 3rd BAK (led by Gen A Z Karavatskiy) to be honoured with Guards titling. The regiment subsequently fought during the battle for the Kursk Salient, as well as in the battles for Sevsk, Gomel and Rechitsa.

During these campaigns, as a rule, crews would drop their bombs in level flight from medium altitudes and in overcast conditions – usually underneath the bottom edge of the clouds. Crews were well versed in carrying out concentrated group attacks, but individual pilots would also make full use of the Pe-2's proven abilities as a dive-bomber.

The tactical and combat skills of the commanders and rank-and-file aviators in 96th GvBAP grew throughout 1943, and this was recognised via the conferring of awards on aircrew who had distinguished themselves – no fewer than nine aviators became Heroes of the Soviet Union whilst serving with the regiment.

96th GvBAP, along with the rest of 3rd BAK, ended the war by participating in the Berlin operation. This began on 16 April 1945 with a mass attack by the Workers' and Peasants' Red Army. The enemy put up fierce resistance – anti-aircraft artillery fire was intense, and Bf 109s and Fw 190s furiously attacked the bombers whenever they could, targeting stragglers in particular. 96th GvBAP lost two aircraft, but hit its targets nevertheless. On 24 April 96th GvBAP became the first unit in 3rd BAK to bomb the German capital.

114th GvBAP

5th SAP (*Smeshannyy Aviatsionniy Polk* – Combined Air Regiment) was formed in September 1939 at an airfield near Murmansk, and it was equipped with I-15bis and I-16 fighters and SB bombers. The regiment came under the control of the Air Forces of 14th Army. Following the outbreak of the Winter War with Finland, two regiments drawn from 5th SAP were formed – 147th IAP, which operated the fighters, and 5th SBAP, which received DB-3 and SB bombers. The regiment was awarded the order of the Red Banner for its distinguished combat against the Finns, and was subsequently re-designated 137th SBAP.

When Germany invaded the USSR on 22 June 1941, 137th SBAP, under Col I D Udonin, was based at Afrikanda. It went to war equipped with 35 SBs, the regiment then receiving its first two Pe-2s from 72nd SBAP in mid July. 137th SBAP was engaged in active combat from the first days of the war, carrying out bombing raids against enemy forces behind the frontline, and bombing the airfields at Rovaniemi and Kemiyarvi in particular in June-July. On 24 July a group of nine SBs successfully bombed a concentration of enemy forces on the hill at Yugon-Veselskya whilst supporting troops from 14th Army. By the end of August the regiment had lost four SBs in combat with enemy fighters and one to flak, 19 aircraft had failed to return from their sorties for unknown reasons and a further 12 were destroyed at Afrikanda in strikes by enemy aircraft. In all 57 aircrew had been killed.

On 26 August two Pe-2s took off to bomb a bridge close to Salmijarvi. Although they failed to reach their intended target, the bombers did destroy a building housing up to 300 enemy troops with a direct hit. On 17 October a group of nine SBs bombed both Alakurtii airfield and the nearby railway station in a surprise attack. The results of this raid were recorded by aerial photography, and it transpired that a bomb dump on the eastern side of the airfield had been destroyed, while a single station building and an ammunition train had also been hit.

Owing to a shortage of aircraft it was necessary now and again to repair badly damaged bombers straight away at the site of an emergency landing. On one occasion a Pe-2 of 137th SBAP had sunk in a freshwater lake after force landing. G M Narbut, a pilot from the Special Air Group of the Civil Air Fleet, was sent to search for it. By flying at low altitude and then landing on the lake in an amphibious aircraft, Narbut hoped to be able to see the submerged aircraft, but his search proved fruitless as he could not see the bottom of the lake. Only with the help of a local forester was the bomber's location determined. A group of divers, together with technical staff led by I N Moiseenko, then raised the Pe-2 to the surface with the help of rubber pontoons and towed it to the shore.

The winter then set in and the job of restoring the aircraft to airworthiness had to be done during the polar night in blizzards and freezing conditions. In spite of all the difficulties and deprivation the technical staff managed to make the aircraft serviceable, and it was soon returned to its airfield.

At the start of the winter in late 1941 a group of Pe-2s arrived to augment the air forces of the Karelian Front. At this point it was decided by the Air Forces of 14th Army that there were sufficient Pe-2s to develop a second regiment with a cadre of 137th SBAP aircrew and technical staff at its core. 608th SBAP was duly formed, the unit soon specialising in photo-reconnaissance. A flight of field-modified Pe-2s carried out this mission, with aircrew being led by Capt S I Stratichevskiy.

April 1942 turned out to be one of the most intensive months of military action in the north. Troops from 14th Army, together with the Northern fleet, were preparing for an offensive. Soviet aviation was mobilised to strike enemy airfields and to photograph its defensive sectors through reconnaissance flights. As part of the offensive 15 Pe-2s of 608th SBAP and eight SBs of 137th SBAP took off on the morning of 23 April, escorted by 20 fighters, and raided enemy airfields at Hebukten and Luostari. The Pe-2s bombed Hebukten with impunity and returned home successfully, but SBs targeting Luostari encountered intensive flak. One bomber was damaged and made an emergency landing close to Pulozero.

On 29 September 1942 nine Pe-2s, led by the commander of 608th SBAP, flew to a forward airfield and then took off on a mission later that same day. After the starboard engine of Snr Lt A M Shchetinin's aircraft

A crew from 96th GvBAP pose near their aeroplane, which carries the inscription *Stalingrad-Berlin*. The regiment's whole combat record appears to be written on the bomber's rear fuselage! The central figure in this photograph is squadron navigator Capt Andrey Krupin, who was awarded the title of Hero of the Soviet Union on 1 May 1943

In the harsh conditions of the Soviet north, reindeers were used to transport bombs to Pe-2s of 114th GvBAP. This regiment became famous through its participation in countless combat operations against German and Finnish forces in this theatre, and it ended the war with the title of Kirkenes Red-Banner and Kutuzov Order regiment, commanded by Maj A N Volodin

suffered a direct hit from a shell, it started to bank sharply to the right. The pilot managed to level the bomber off and began flying the aircraft back to base on one engine, but this too gave out after only a few kilometres. The area in which he was forced to make an emergency landing was covered in forest, and Shchetinin and his crew were not found until eight days later. Starving from hunger and suffering from injuries caused in the crash-landing, they were met by a partisan who led them back to his regiment.

In November 1942, owing to a shortage of reinforcements, the command decided to merge 137th and 608th SBAPs into a single regiment under the command of Maj V V Kotov. The combined unit was designated 137th SBAP, the regiment's former commander, Col I D Udonin, being promoted to lead 260th BAD.

In early March 1943 the homogenous aviation divisions of 7th Air Army on the Karelian Front were re-formed into mixed divisions by order of the People's Commissariat for Defence. 137th SBAP was transferred to 258th SAD at this time, and six months later, on 24 August 1943, the division became 1st GvSAD. 137th SBAP also changed designation to 114th GvBAP by order of the People's Commissariat for Defence of the USSR.

By 20 June 1944 the regiment had been deployed to the area around the River Svir, where it participated in the Svir-Petrozavodsk operation, attacking enemy columns and reinforcements. During one such mission, on 27 June, two squadrons from 114th GvBAP targeted Finnish artillery batteries. The first wave of nine aircraft, led by Capt A M Shchetinin, destroyed several gun emplacements. The second wave of nine, led by Maj Ya E Nikolayev, appeared over the target 40 minutes later. So as to achieve the element of surprise, crews had throttled back the engines of their Pe-2s and coasted in over the batteries. It was later established from aerial camera footage that 24 vehicles and several gun emplacements were destroyed and up to 150 Finnish soldiers killed.

In October 1944 114th GvBAP supported advancing Soviet forces during the Petsamo-Kirkenes offensive. In recognition of its active role in the routing of the enemy and the liberation of the town of Kirkenes, 114th GvBAP, under Maj A N Volodin, was awarded the honorary title of 'Kirkenes' via an order from Supreme High Command.

GUARDS BOMBER AIR DIVISIONS

In the spring of 1942 Lieutenant-General of Aviation A A Novikov became the new commander-in-chief of the VVS RKKA. He was one of the initiators of reform in the organisational structure of the air force, during which the air forces at the fronts were transformed into air armies. Each air army would incorporate several air divisions, as well as independent regiments and squadrons. As a result of these changes the so-called 'army complements' of air forces were eradicated. Until the reforms almost every general-purpose army had its own air force (more often than not a Combined Air Division or several independent regiments).

The majority of the new air divisions were formed for these air armies in the spring of 1942, and they were homogenous in their makeup, consisting of either fighter, ground attack or bomber units. However, there were on occasion Combined Air Divisions too.

The Headquarters of Supreme High Command also created special reserve formations (air divisions and air corps) that it could 'issue' to the front when needed, together with their constituent air armies. These reserve units were formed because the High Command was unable to secure sufficient forces and equipment for military action on all fronts (the principle being 'always have something in reserve'). After an offensive or defensive action on a specific front had been completed, these formations could be withdrawn and transferred to a different sector. The Supreme High Command's reserve air divisions were homogenous as a rule, but the air corps were often mixed (for example, two divisions of ground attack aircraft and one of fighters).

The numbering system for air divisions also changed, as did their organisational structure. Thus, the year 1942 came first, followed by the first digit of a three-digit number and then a two-digit serial number. The numbering system started with 1st Air Army, which had been deployed to the Western Front. It was here that the first bomber air division of the 'new formation' was founded, 204th BAD.

Brothers-in-arms lift up their anonymous crew commander following a successful sortie on his 20th birthday

3rd GvBAD

In April 1942 a decree arrived in Kondrovo, where the headquarters of 146th BAD was located – this division had been deployed to the base, home of 6th RAG, in November 1941. It ordered the redeployment of the division's command post to the village of Aduyevo, east of Medyn, and stated that the unit was to re-form as 204th BAD, with new personnel. In this case the previous divisional commander, Col L G Kuldin, was promoted and made deputy chief of staff of 1st Air Army. The headquarters never moved to the new location, however, as another decree arrived ordering it to redeploy to Kubinka, in Podmoskov'ye.

By the end of May 1942, 2nd, 6th and 130th SBAPs had been transferred to 204th BAD control, and 38th and 261st SBAPs subsequently joined this formation too. All were equipped with Pe-2 dive-bombers. Military commissar Col L A Dubrovin served with the division from its formation, and he recalled;

'Up until that point I had served in mixed formations handling different aircraft types close to the frontline, where the artillery batteries could just be heard. Upon my transfer to 204th BAD I became a bomber pilot, and with my fellow aviators, I found myself a few dozen kilometres away from the frontline. My comrades and I all felt that we were perhaps too far into the rear, as we could no longer hear the artillery. This, however, turned out to be a false impression, for the war quickly reached us. Towards the end of my first week with the division our airfield was subjected to a raid by 14 Junkers aircraft, as a result of which the division lost a Pe-2.'

On 1 June 1942 Hero of the Soviet Union Col V A Ushakov joined the headquarters, having received orders to head 204th BAD. According to the memoirs of veterans in this formation, he knew the specifics of crew training, detachments and bomber aviation units well, excelled in piloting the Pe-2 and possessed decisiveness, integrity and, at that time, reasonable caution. Ushakov played an important role in building the formation, participating personally in combat sorties. This proved to be critically important as many of the aircrews were young and unseasoned. Ushakov relied on his experienced commanders, including Majs M I Martynov and V I Dymchenko and Capts G M Markov, A A Lokhanov and D I Butkov.

204th BAD's first combat sortie was flown on 1 June when six Pe-2s from 6th BAP, under the command of Capt Petrovets, bombed the German airfield at Seshcha, escorted by fighters from 46th IAK (*Istrebitel'nyy Aviatsionnyy Korpus* – Fighter Aviation Corps). This sortie was deemed to be successful.

The raids on airfields and railway junctions, as well as aerial reconnaissance sorties, met with resistance from enemy fighters, and the missions themselves were often hampered by unsettled weather. To avoid wasteful losses, intensive training began within the regiments, time for this being found between sorties and in the evenings. Classroom theory was covered during periods of bad weather. The divisional commander issued an order stating that only regimental commanders and navigators were to deliver the training personally, together with squadron commanders. As a result, losses among flight crew in the first three months of combat were comparatively low.

During an attack on a column of German tanks at Rzhev on 7 August the group was led by the division's military commissar, Col L A Dubrovin. His aircraft was hit by anti-aircraft fire while approaching the target, and after his bombing run he became detached from the formation and was pounced upon by a Bf 109. Dubrovin's Pe-2 eventually managed to escape the fighters, but not before the bomber had been set on fire. Navigator military commissar senior political leader M M Chernov had also been mortally wounded.

Having crossed back into Soviet-held territory, Dubrovin and radio-operator/gunner Sgt K F Frolov managed to bail out, but Chernov was unable to escape the burning aircraft and perished when it crashed. The following day Dubrovin and Frolov returned to their airfield. Navigator Snr Sgt V M Klyagin, whose Pe-2 had been shot down at almost the same time as they were, also failed to return.

On several occasions over the summer months Ju 88 bombers attacked 204th BAD's airfield. One such raid nearly caused a calamity when a Junkers bomber set an idling, fully armed and fuelled Pe-2 on fire. Had the aircraft exploded, other 'Peshkas' loaded with fuel and bombs could have easily followed suit. However, Lieutenant-technician T M Sizov displayed great heroism and courage when he ran out to the burning bomber. With the help of technicians Yakushin and Usov, he taxied the aircraft to the far side of the airfield and then shut down its engines. A few minutes later it exploded, but nobody was hurt and no other aircraft were damaged.

In carrying out Stalin's dreaded order number 227, issued in July 1942 and known in the Red Army as 'not one step back', a so-called 'punishment squadron' was introduced among the personnel in the division. The thinking of 1st Air Army Command was that pilots, navigators and gunners who committed violations would be sent to see out the rest of their service in the most dangerous sectors of the front, where they would be given the most difficult objectives so as to teach them courage and bravery. The commissars emphasised this – the guilty had to cleanse themselves of the mark of shame with their own blood.

One such punishment squadron was set up within 261st SBAP, and those officers who had given an excellent account of themselves (Capt P D Osipenko, Military Commissar Senior Political Leader I G Petrov and navigator 2Lt M S Kozhemyakin) were to lead the unit. As a reward, they were given an increase in pay and their length of service was counted twice as fast as other veteran servicemen. However, not a single airman was ever sent to the punishment squadron, as the following note in 204th BAD's political report during the winter of 1942-43 explains;

'There are no pilots, navigators or radio-operator/gunners in the regiments under this division who are guilty of cowardice, selfishness or sabotage. Thus nobody has been sent to the punishment squadron.'

One of 1st Air Army command's key tactics during this period was to routinely target enemy airfields. In early autumn 1942 an operation was planned to destroy enemy materiel on the airfield near the Dugino collective farm. On 3 September three groups of 'Peshkas' bombed the airfield and the aprons, and according to reports from the crews 30-35 enemy aircraft were put out of action.

With the onset of severe weather in late 1942, combat along the Western Front tailed off. Making the most of this quiet period, 204th BAD set up an unauthorised training centre with the aim of improving flying training for newly arrived aircrew. The school was to play a decisive role in teaching pilots how to master the art of dive-bombing. Insufficient attention had been paid to this mode of operation for the Pe-2 at training centres in the rear, mostly because of a lack of fuel.

On 3 September 1942 130th SBAP of 204th BAD participated in an attack on the enemy airfield at Sovkhoz Dugino. According to the crews' reports, 30-35 German aeroplanes were destroyed. These airmen are conducting an impromptu brief for the benefit of the photographer prior to participating in the mission

 (text continues on page 43)

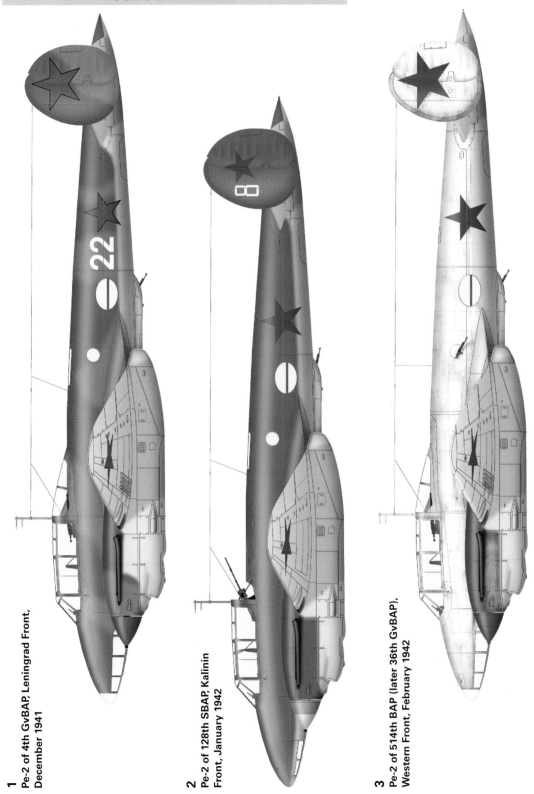

1
Pe-2 of 4th GvBAP, Leningrad Front,
December 1941

2
Pe-2 of 128th SBAP, Kalinin
Front, January 1942

3
Pe-2 of 514th BAP (later 36th GvBAP),
Western Front, February 1942

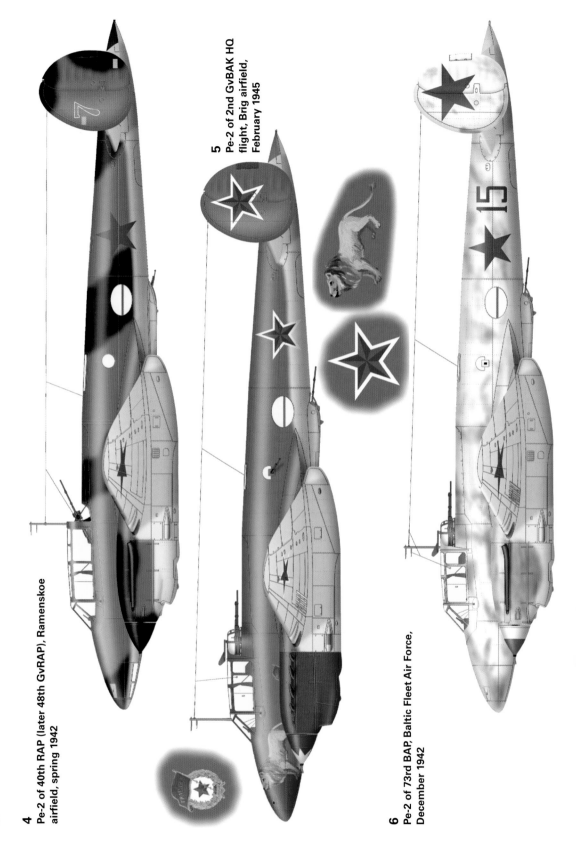

4
Pe-2 of 40th RAP (later 48th GvRAP), Ramenskoe airfield, spring 1942

5
Pe-2 of 2nd GvBAK HQ flight, Brig airfield, February 1945

6
Pe-2 of 73rd BAP, Baltic Fleet Air Force, December 1942

7
Pe-2 of 12th GvBAP,
Baltic Fleet Air Force,
November 1944

8
UPe-2 of 12th GvBAP,
Baltic Fleet Air Force,
May 1944

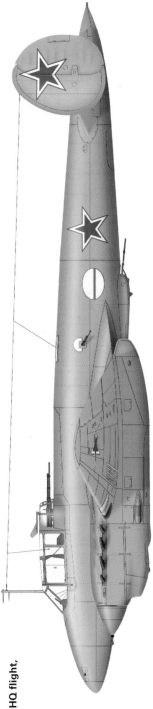

9
Pe-2 of 2nd GvBAK HQ flight,
Austria, May 1945

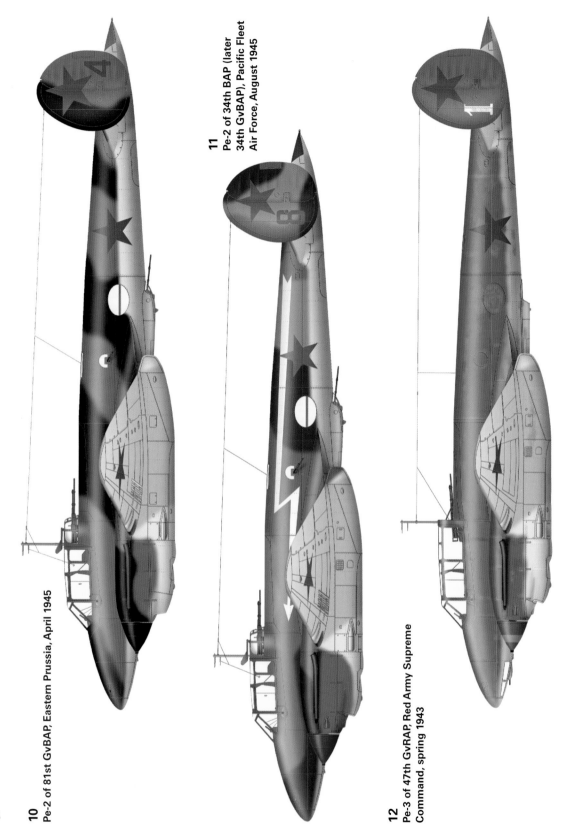

10
Pe-2 of 81st GvBAP, Eastern Prussia, April 1945

11
Pe-2 of 34th BAP (later 34th GvBAP), Pacific Fleet Air Force, August 1945

12
Pe-3 of 47th GvRAP, Red Army Supreme Command, spring 1943

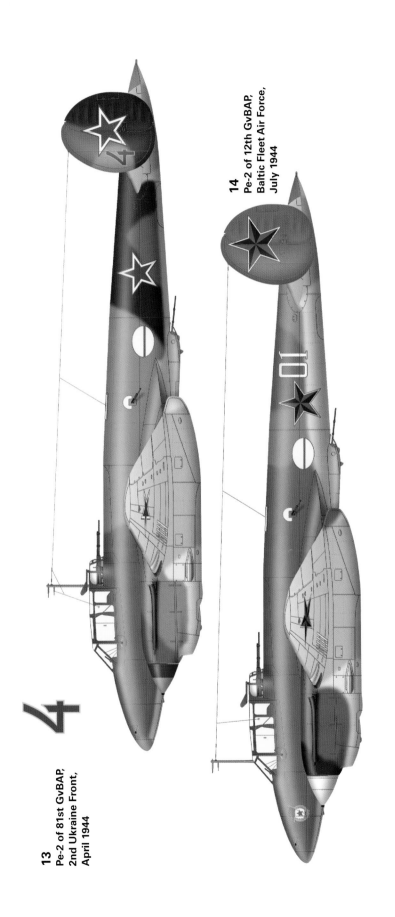

13
Pe-2 of 81st GvBAP,
2nd Ukraine Front,
April 1944

14
Pe-2 of 12th GvBAP,
Baltic Fleet Air Force,
July 1944

15
Pe-2 of 261st SBAP, Voronejscky Front,
August 1943

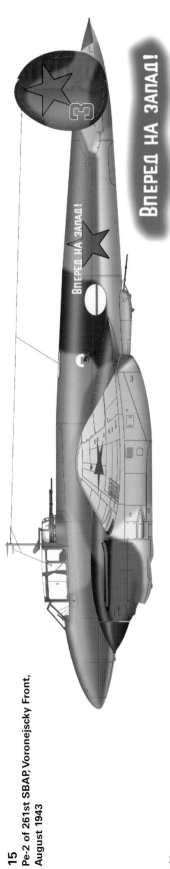

ВПЕРЕД НА ЗАПАД!

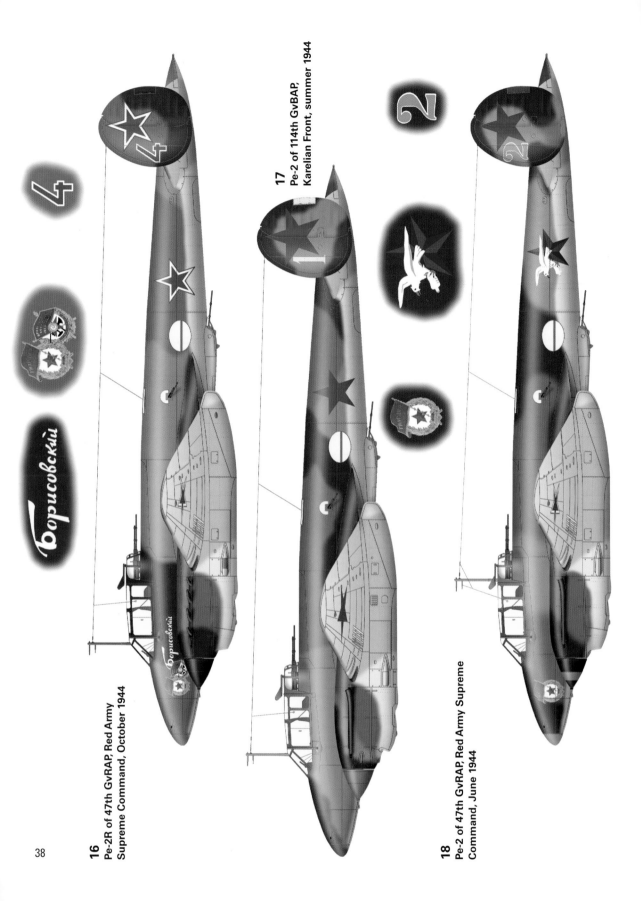

16
Pe-2R of 47th GvRAP, Red Army
Supreme Command, October 1944

17
Pe-2 of 114th GvBAP,
Karelian Front, summer 1944

18
Pe-2 of 47th GvRAP, Red Army Supreme
Command, June 1944

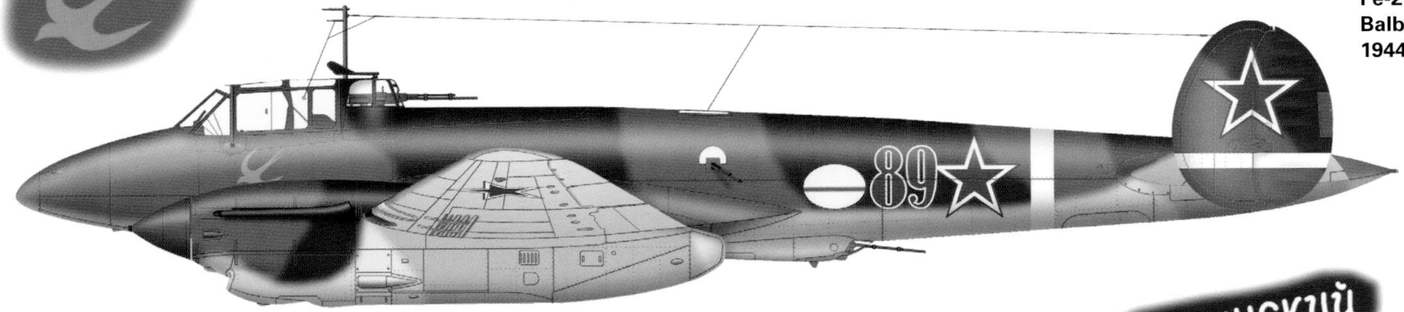

19
Pe-2 of 125th GvBAP,
Balbasovo airfield, July
1944

Берлинский

20
Pe-2 of 82nd GvBAP, 2nd Ukraine
Front, June 1944

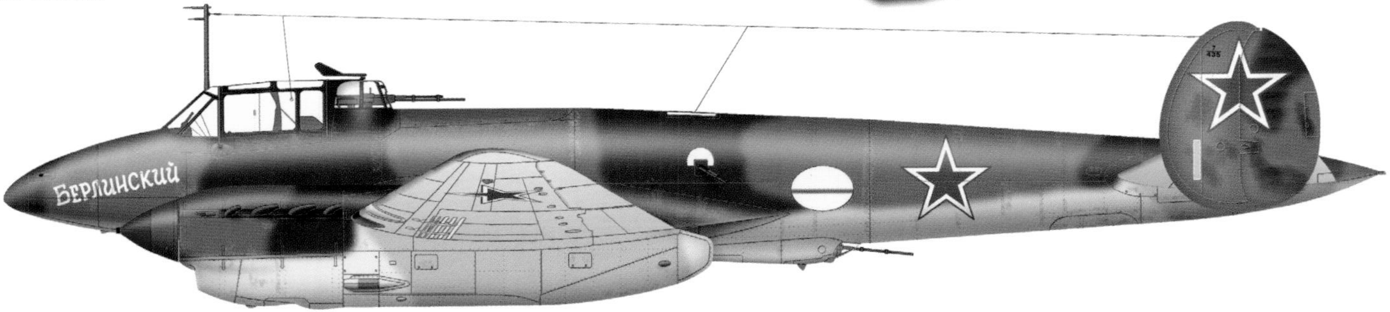

Берлинский

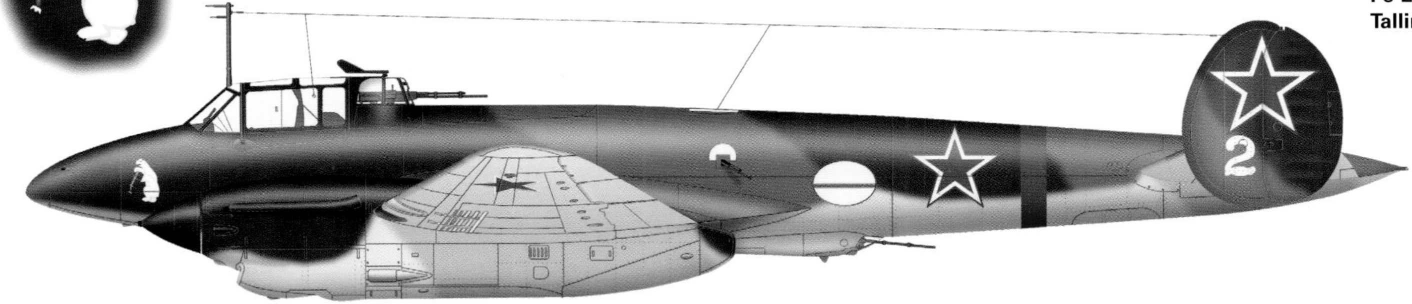

21
Pe-2 of 140th SBAP,
Tallinn region, August 1944

39

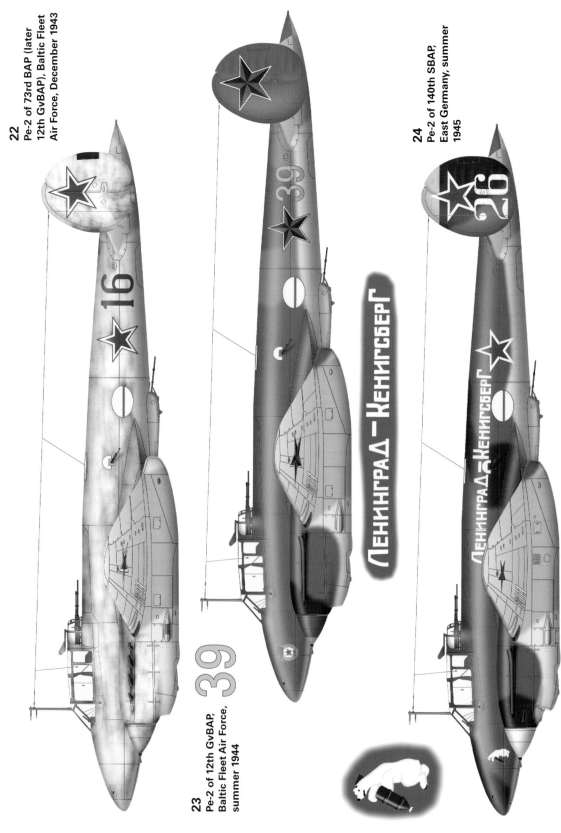

22
Pe-2 of 73rd BAP (later 12th GvBAP), Baltic Fleet Air Force, December 1943

23
Pe-2 of 12th GvBAP, Baltic Fleet Air Force, summer 1944

24
Pe-2 of 140th SBAP, East Germany, summer 1945

25
Pe-2 of 162nd GvBAP,
Ukraine, August 1943

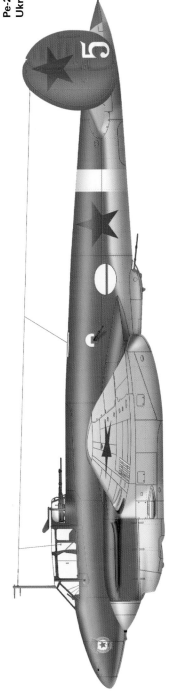

26
Pe-2 of 162nd GvBAP, Ukraine,
February 1944

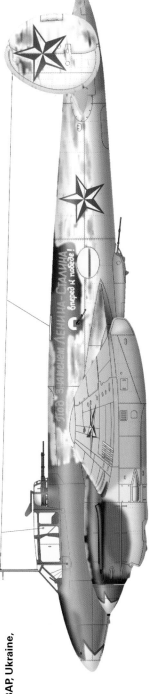

27
Pe-2 of 34th GvBAP,
Karelian Front, July 1944

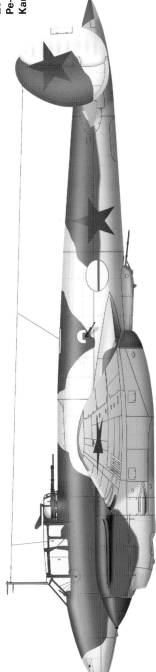

41

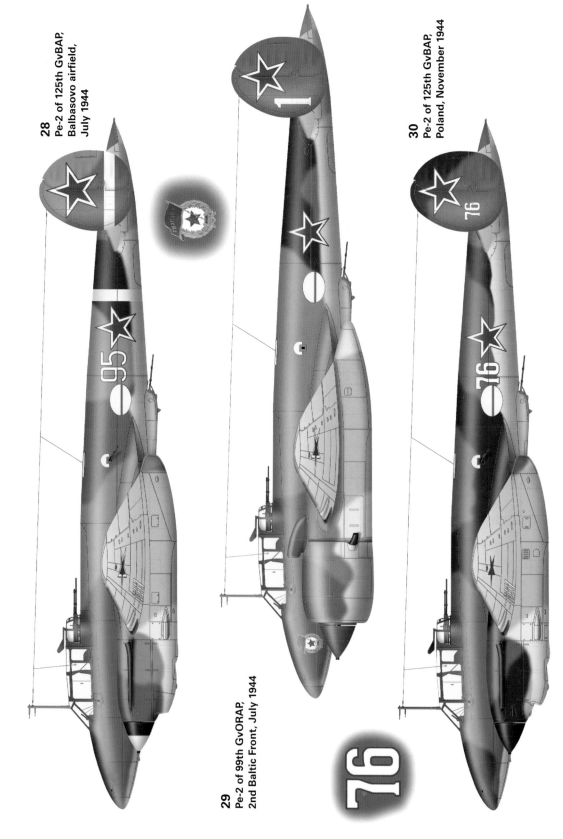

28
Pe-2 of 125th GvBAP,
Balbasovo airfield,
July 1944

29
Pe-2 of 99th GvORAP,
2nd Baltic Front, July 1944

30
Pe-2 of 125th GvBAP,
Poland, November 1944

At the end of January 1943 Col V A Ushakov, who had been promoted to general, moved on to a new posting and the division was taken over by Col S P Andreyev, who had previously served in the Workers' and Peasants' Red Army Inspectorate. Aside from the units equipped with 'Peshkas', 204th BAD also controlled 179th IAP (flying Hurricanes), 22nd GvBAP (flying SBs) and 21st Reconnaissance Air Squadron (flying Su-2s).

The enemy made good use of this pause in operations, Luftwaffe pilots studying the merits and shortcomings of Soviet aircraft as they sought ways to counter them effectively. One of the key changes was the introduction of well-armed Fw 190A fighters to this theatre.

On 23 February 1943 – Red Army Day – 204th BAD regiments took to the skies in their entirety following an improvement in the weather. Following combat with Fw 190s and Bf 109s of JG 51, no fewer than 14 Pe-2s from the division failed to return to their airfield. The Germans claimed that 18 bombers had been destroyed. Some of the downed airmen were able to avoid death or capture, including the commander of 261st SBAP, Lt Col M I Martynov, and navigator Capt G I Armashov. They both spent eight days fighting their way back from behind the frontline.

Subsequently, the Supreme Commander of Air Forces, S A Khudyakov, took responsibility for such serious losses among the divisions, stating that on 23 February he had been unable to spare a single fighter to escort the 'Peshkas'.

From early spring 1943 the division contributed to the disruption of rail transport around Smolensk and participated in strikes on enemy airfields. For the latter missions the bombers were escorted by fighters from 303rd IAD (*Istrebitel'naya Aviatsionnaya Diviziya* – Fighter Air Division) and the French 'Normandie' squadron, which was subordinate to it on many sorties.

A morning raid on Seshcha airfield on 6 May by three groups of nine aircraft was successful, taking the enemy by surprise. Two Pe-2s from 2nd and 130th SBAPs were lost in subsequent evening raids, but a mission by two groups of eight aircraft to the airfield at Bryansk was carried out without any losses. However, a catastrophe befell an aircraft of 38th SBAP on that day when a Pe-2 brought back a bomb in its bomb-bay that had failed to release. The weapon exploded on landing, killing 15 people and injuring five more.

Although the daylight raids had, in the main, been successful, a twilight operation against Bryansk on 8 June produced mixed results. Using a plan developed as a result of previous raids, groups of aircraft

2nd SBAP was one of the oldest regiments in the Red Army Air Force, having been established in April 1938 at Soltsy airfield in the Leningrad Military District under Col Boris Pisarskiy. By the beginning of the war the regiment was commanded by Andrey Voloshin as part of 204th BAD. Here, FAB-100 bombs are being transported in wooden containers, which allowed the weapons to be move with greater safety than by dragging or rolling them. This photograph was taken on the Western Front during the severe winter of 1942-43

The commander of 123rd GvBAP, Lt Col M I Martynov (left, in cap), and his deputy in charge of policy congratulate the crew of a Pe-2 after their 50th combat mission. Martynov later became the commander of 3rd GvBAD, his post at 123rd GvBAP being filled by Lt Col V I Dymchenko

from 204th BAD approached the airfield from different directions and at different altitudes at 60- to 90-second intervals. Bombing was carried out in level flight, aiming as per the lead Pe-2. Crews witnessed five direct hits on aircraft, accompanied by pockets of fire and bomb explosions around the aprons, on the runway and among German anti-aircraft positions in the western part of the airfield. A huge explosion was seen on the northwestern side of the airfield following the striking of an ammunition dump.

By the spring of 1943 early series Pe-2s such as the aircraft seen here had become rare birds in 204th SBAP. Side glazing panels in the nose and the absence of the navigator's VUB-1 turret indicate that this 'Peshka' was built not later than spring 1942. Having survived more than a year in combat, veteran aeroplanes such as this one were usually relegated to training duties, although there were exceptions to this rule

Unfortunately the leader of the group from 261st SBAP, Maj I G Petrov, mistakenly turned too tightly en route to the target. As a result his formation broke up and the dive-bombers were forced to regroup as a line of individual aircraft. Petrov's second mistake proved fatal. He was too late in making a manoeuvre to avoid anti-aircraft fire. The first salvo of shells exploded to one side of the Pe-2s, but a 'Peshka' was shot down by the second salvo and the leader's aircraft was also hit by flak – a shell fragment killed Petrov, after which the machine began to lose altitude.

Navigator G I Armashov's presence of mind did not fail him, however, and he managed to move the dead pilot out of the way and take the control yoke himself. Luckily, he possessed some skill when it came to controlling the aircraft. Armashov then dropped the bombs and turned for home. A pair of Fw 190s attacked the 'Peshka' as it withdrew, but gunner Sgt Pukhov repelled the attack, helped by escorting fighters. The navigator had never landed a Pe-2, and taking into account the onset of darkness and the poor low-speed handling characteristics of the dive-bomber, he decided to bail out by parachute, along with the gunner.

Aside from Petrov, 261st SBAP also lost the crews of Sgts D P Struchkov and N A Yerotskiy, their Pe-2s failing to return from this mission.

Three types of bombs are seen under the wing of this Pe-2 of 261st SBAP during the summer of 1943. The armourer to the right is resting his foot on a captured German SC 250, while the nearest bomb is a FAB-100 with a welded body. Behind it are FAB-100s with cast-iron bodies

On 14 September 1943 dive-bombers from 3rd GvBAD carried out a massive attack on Borovsk airfield. Seven nine-aircraft groups of Pe-2s participated in the operation, approaching the target from three directions. Reconnaissance flights over the target in subsequent days indicated that the Luftwaffe lost 50-55 combat aircraft during the attack. This was probably one of the most effective bombing raids ever carried out by the Pe-2. Here, just prior to undertaking the mission, the pilot and navigator of 'white 9' confer over a map of the target area, while the radio-operator/gunner conducts last-minute checks on his 7.62 mm machine gun with the help of an armourer

Later on 10 June Soviet bombers carried out a second raid on Seshcha airfield. The first two groups of nine aircraft dropped their bombs successfully, and attacks by Fw 190s were beaten back with the help of escorting fighters. However, not all of the aircraft from the third group of nine Pe-2s from 6th SBAP, escorted by six La-5s, returned to their airfield. Two Lavochkin fighters were also shot down, together with six of the bombers. On this occasion the numerical advantage enjoyed by the German fighters had influenced the outcome of the raid, as had the unsuccessful tactics employed by 6th SBAP's formation leader. The latter had only converted to the 'Peshka' one month before the raid, having previously flown the Polikarpov U-2 biplane. Of the 18 bomber aircrew shot down on the 10th, only 1Lt N T Smolskiy escaped with his life.

Over the course of two summer days (8 and 10 June) 204th BAD had flown 71 combat sorties (62 against Seshcha airfield and nine against Bryansk) and lost 15 Pe-2s, 12 of which were shot down by German fighters.

During subsequent combat over the Kursk Salient 204th BAD units made use of a large group rendezvous in a circle for the first time, the formation then meeting up with escorting fighters 'head on' without having initially performed the traditional circuit of their airfield. One of the most successful raids of this period was against Beliya Berega railway station on 17 June, which was targeted by four groups of nine bombers. Tracks and station buildings were destroyed and two trains were set on fire, disrupting movements in the Orel-Bryansk sector for days. When reconnaissance crews confirmed the effectiveness of the strike, the commander of the Red Army Air Force, Marshal A A Novikov, expressed his gratitude to all the participants. It is noteworthy that the division did not incur any losses among its personnel during the raid on the railway station or throughout the whole of July 1943.

Following an intense August imbued with action, in which the division fought first in the direction of Bolkhovsk and later Smolensk, 6th and 38th SBAPs were withdrawn from the formation for augmentation. 204th BAD had flown 898 combat sorties in a month and dropped 645 tonnes (635 tons) of bombs. 179th IAP, 22nd GBAP and 21st Reconnaissance Air Squadron attached to the division had been withdrawn even earlier. The loss of these units left the division with just 70 serviceable and ten unserviceable Pe-2s, and 46 crews, at combat readiness in the three remaining regiments.

Joyful news arrived on 3 September 1943, however, as the division had been re-designated 3rd GvBAD as a reward for its exploits over the previous year. The units remaining in the division also became Guards regiments, 2nd SBAP changing to 119th GvBAP, 130th SBAP becoming 122nd GvBAP and 261st SBAP being re-designated 123rd GvBAP. The deputy commander of 1st Air Army, Gen A K Bogorodetskiy, duly awarded the commanders of these units, Lt Cols S N Gavrilov and V I Dymchenko and Maj N K Zaytsev, Guards colours.

Eleven days later 1st Air Army headquarters tasked the division with attacking the airfield at Vorovskoye, where, according to information from military intelligence, a large number of German aircraft were based. Four groups of nine bombers, led by 123rd GvBAP CO Maj V I Dymchenko, were despatched. Dense cloud cover en route to the target forced crews to descend to an altitude of 700-800 m (2300-2600 ft) before making their bombing runs, and they were able to deliver their ordnance accurately. A subsequent raid, led by the commander of 122nd GvBAP, Lt Col S N Gavrilov, took place as the day drew to a close.

According to Soviet figures the enemy lost 55-60 aircraft, and not less than 100 soldiers. German reports state that the *Stukageschwader* operating from the airfield temporarily lost its combat capability after as many as 20 of its Ju 87s were destroyed. 3rd GvBAD losses during these raids amounted to two Pe-2s.

In total the division flew 451 bombing raids in September, losing seven aircraft in combat and a further three Pe-2s in accidents.

Combat sorties, victories and losses – this was how things were for 3rd GvBAD on the Western Front as it participated in the biggest operations in the second half of the war. Judging by the documentation for the unit, despite it being adversely affected by an acute lack of fuel in the second half of July 1944, the division succeeded in accomplishing a great deal, and moreover it did it without incurring heavy losses. 'The division supported troops on the 3rd Belarusian Front in taking the cities of Borisov, Vileyka, Minsk and Vilnius, and also in crossing the river Neman', one report pointed out, adding '119th and 122th GvBAPs became red banner regiments on 10 July 1944'.

Despite flying 422 sorties in August 1944, the division lost just three 'Peshkas' – all were shot down by a lone Fw 190 that suddenly attacked a group of bombers in the evening twilight.

At the beginning of September 3rd GvBAD was withdrawn from 1st Air Army's line-up, moved away to Supreme Command Headquarters and was then made operationally subordinate to 16th Air Army on the Belarusian Front. The division did not remain under 16th Air Army control for very long, however, for at the end of October it was redeployed to the Siauliai region of Lithuania. It was here that troops from the 1st Baltic Front set about eradicating enemy forces that had been pulled back from East Prussia. 3rd GvBAD duly became part of 3rd Air Army.

Seeing considerable action on this front through to VE Day, 3rd GvBAD ended the war on the shores of the Baltic, assisting troops from the 3rd Belarusian Front to take Konigsberg and Pillau.

This camouflaged Pe-2 was flown by the commander of 135th GvBAP, Lt Col D D Valentik. Note the letter 'K' on the fin. The bomber also has yellow fin tips. Dmitriy Valentik initially distinguished himself during the Winter War against Finland in 1939-40, earning him the award of Hero of the Soviet Union. He then flew 115 combat sorties in Pe-2s during the Great Patriotic War, leading bomber groups on the most important missions. Valentik was duly nominated for a second award of Hero of the Soviet Union, although this was not ratified. From December 1944 he held the post of deputy commander of 6th GvBAD, his CO in this unit being his friend Lt Col Fedor Paliy

Pilot Snr Lt N D Panasov (right), radio-operator/gunner Snr Sgt Savchuk (left) and navigator Snr Lt Makhonko (rear centre) served as a crew with 140th SBAP from operations in defence of Leningrad to the final assault on eastern Germany. The inscription *'Leningrad-Kenigsberg'* on the fuselage of the bomber indicates the crew's combat history

The crew of Hero of the Soviet Union A P Malin (centre) in front of their bomber. During the war Anatoliy Malin, who served with 140th SBAP on the Tallinn front, completed 182 combat sorties. Note the Pe-2's nose art – a white bear holding a bomb. All 'Peshkas' assigned to 140th SBAP featured this marking

6th GvBAD

According to an order from the commander of the South-Western Front, Marshal S K Timoshenko, following receipt of a corresponding directive from Supreme High Command headquarters, 270th BAD commenced formation on 11 May 1942. The division was created on the basis that 4th RAG and, initially, 52nd, 135th and 826th SBAPs would become part of it (the latter three units all flew the Su-2 bomber, their commanders being Majs A I Pushkin, G M Korzinshchikov and A M Bokun, respectively). 94th SBAP, led by Col A P Nikolayev, was also assigned to the new division, this unit being equipped with the Pe-2.

The division was led by Col S A Yegorov, who had previously commanded 99th SBAP. Having converted onto the Pe-2 shortly before the German invasion of the USSR, Yegorov rated the aircraft's speed (appreciably higher than other Soviet medium bombers at that time), the durability of its construction and its enormous potential.

270th BAD commenced military action on 12 June, the division coming under the control of 8th Air Army, led by the Major-General of Aviation, T T Khryukin – one of Stalin's young protégés, he was just 32 years old. The unit was committed to combat in the aerial battles fought over the great bend in the Don River, these being particularly ferocious after 28 June when the Wehrmacht began a general offensive along the southern sector of the Soviet-German Front.

VVS RKKA units rapidly lost equipment and personnel, and one air regiment had to be hastily replaced by another. At the beginning of July 94th SBAP departed for the rear and 99th 'Yegorov' SBAP, led by Maj A Yu Yakobson, took up arms in its place. Soon it was necessary to withdraw those regiments equipped with Su-2s from the frontline as industry had halted production of the bomber, and replacing growing losses with aircraft that had just been repaired became unrealistic during this period of intensive activity.

There was, however, a shortage of Pe-2s as well, and their numbers within 270th BAD at this time rarely exceeded 20-25 combat-ready aircraft. Divisional commander S A Yegorov subsequently received 275th, 797th and 140th SBAPs, equipped with 'Peshkas' from the training units to replace the division's Su-2 regiments. Unfortunately, these new units were predominantly staffed by

47

young aircrews. And in a combat environment where the enemy enjoyed air supremacy around Stalingrad, coupled with a lack of escorting fighters, they incurred grievous losses that saw the regiments rapidly lose their combat readiness. For example, 797th SBAP under Maj G G Bystrov arrived on 15 August and had to be pulled back to Kazan to regroup just ten days later.

It was particularly badly hit on 20 August, which proved to be one of the blackest days in the history of 270th BAD as a whole. Of the 60 crews that took off on a mission to attack German crossing points over the Don, only 51 reached the target and 14 Pe-2s were lost. None of the first group of nine bombers returned from the raid (these 'Peshkas' belonged to 797th BAP, and they were supposed to carry out raids around Trekhostrovskiy, Nizhniy Akatov and Gerasimov). It soon became clear that German fighters had shot down all nine aircraft. Six airmen, including the pilot of the lead machine, Regimental Commander G G Bystrov (who the day before had been promoted to the rank of lieutenant colonel), were able to use their parachutes and subsequently returned to the unit. A further six were rescued, having suffered burns or trauma, and seven were killed in action in their aircraft. The fate of the remaining eight is unknown.

Owing to an acute lack of fighters, 8th Air Army command decided to relieve them of the need to escort bombers during the day, concentrating all their efforts on the battle for aerial supremacy over Stalingrad and the interception of enemy bombers and ground attack aircraft. Without any escorts to protect them, aircrew from 270th BAD were instructed to increase the operating altitude of their Pe-2s to 7500-8000 metres (24,600-26,200 ft), where Bf 109s were less active. Nevertheless, 'Peshka' crews had to overcome enormous difficulties during literally every sortie in order to complete their missions and return safely.

For example, on 8 September Sgt A A Zabotin's aircraft from 275th SBAP was damaged by flak 130 km (80 miles) from the frontline. Having dropped his bombs on target, he then managed to nurse the Pe-2 back to the Volga on just one engine, landing in a field on the eastern side of the river.

Enemy resistance grew a little weaker during October and Soviet aviation losses reduced as a result. However, at this time enemy fighters began to intercept high-flying Pe-2s more frequently. Snr Lt A I Usov's crew failed to return on 3 October, and three days later the crews of Snr Lts V V Levchenko and G S Malakhovich were also lost. On 7 October Snr Lt F A Zeleneyev's aircraft was shot down while flying at an altitude of 7600 m (24,900 ft). In an effort to prevent further losses, Pe-2 crews changed the direction of their approach to the target and made better use of cloud cover when on their bombing runs.

Units tasked with long-range photo-reconnaissance also started sending out Pe-2s in pairs so as to improve their defensive capabilities – it was easier for two 'Peshkas' to beat off attacks by Bf 109s and Bf 110s than one.

Crews from 270th BAD played a key role in the counterattack outside Stalingrad, which began on 19 November 1942. The most important events took place in extraordinarily difficult weather conditions, with blizzards and snowstorms greatly limiting visibility. Soviet forces broke through the enemy's defences at its flanks with groups of mechanised cavalry, and had surrounded the principal forces of the German 6th Field Army in the space of just a few days. The weather was not very favourable for flying until mid-December, however, with the most active aviation units at that time flying U-2 biplanes – these were used to impede the progress of German troop reserves heading for the front, the U-2 nuisance raiders doing their part to disrupt the regrouping of the Wehrmacht. Pe-2 crews from 270th BAD eventually joined the fighting from 12 December onwards following an improvement in the weather.

Initially, the German opposition to the offensive was quite weak, but within a few days the enemy had strengthened its defences around railway junctions by keeping fighters on patrol overhead. On 18-19 December the bombers had to break through a shield of both anti-aircraft artillery and Bf 109s in order to reach enemy trains. Snr Sgt V S Pimonov's crew from 284th SBAP took up the fight on leaving the target, radio-operator/gunner A M Tucha and gunner/bombardier M P Frolov beating off two attacks by enemy fighters that closed to within 50 metres (160 ft). They were both killed when the aircraft made a third pass, which also set the bomber's main fuel tank alight as it overflew Aksay. It was at this point that Pimonov was forced to bail out. That same day 2Lt A F Kurochkin's crew failed to return from a mission against enemy troops defending Gremyachiy Farm.

On 20 December, a series of tough tests awaited the crew of a Pe-2 that took off on a reconnaissance mission to photograph German reserve units in Gremyachiy, Generalovskiy and Kotelnikovo. Having overflown the designated target areas, the navigator, Snr Sgt Tsaplin, informed the pilot, Snr Sgt Prozvanchenikov, that he could now head for home. Moments later the 'Peshka' was attacked from different directions by several Bf 109s. While Snr Sgt Dmitriyev returned fire with a machine gun, Snr Sgt Tsaplin relayed the results of the mission to the command post in plain text.

The aircraft's fuel tanks soon caught fire, and the navigator and gunner were fatally wounded. Attempts to extinguish the fire by diving proved unsuccessful, so Prozvanchenikov jettisoned his canopy and bailed out. Opening his parachute at low altitude, he survived a heavy landing and eventually returned to his regiment on horseback. He had suffered burns to his face and hands, but once these had healed he rejoined 270th BAD.

The operation to rout the enemy formations at Kotelnikovo, in which 270th BAD participated during the second half of December, ultimately proved to be successful. Controlled by 8th Air Army, bombers from the division inflicted heavy casualties on German troops fighting around Rostov from 24 January 1943. Morale amongst Soviet airmen at this time was excellent, and the fate of the encircled German 6th Army was no longer in doubt. The Wehrmacht had

A young Pe-2 crew prepares for a combat mission during the summer of 1943. Their aircraft carries the inscription *For Stalin!*. The navigator and pilot are both junior lieutenants, having graduated from a flying school no more than two or three months previously, while the radio-operator/gunner, on the right, is a sergeant. None have earned any bravery awards as yet

suffered its first, and heaviest, defeat in the east. For the airmen of 270th BAD, news of the surrender of Field Marshal Friedrich Paulus and his forces on 2 February 1943 coincided with other news. Col G A Guchev was to replace Col S A Yegorov as divisional commander (Yegorov was later to command 8th RAB, which trained pilots to fly the 'Peshka').

The division's subsequently participated in the liberation of Donbass (Donetsk), troops on the Southern Front starting the Miusskaya offensive

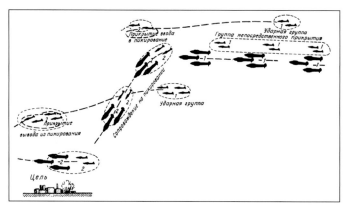

This period drawing from a VVS RKKA tactics manual shows a typical dive-bombing strike by a Pe-2 group with fighter coverage. The fighters would be split into three groups, namely a direct escort group, a strike group at the altitude at which the dive was entered and a strike group at the altitude at which the dive was exited. When implemented correctly, an attack such as this would create serious problems for defending Bf 109 and Fw 190 pilots

on 17 June 1943. Along with the entire 8th Air Army, the regiments of 270th BAD went into battle in support of them.

By then the composition of the division had stabilised – 86th and 284th SBAPs flew Pe-2s and 10th GvBAP was equipped with A-20Bs. As a rule, during the Miusskaya offensive the regiments equipped with Pe-2s operated in daylight, taking off on sorties in groups of nine, and the A-20B regiment flew in the evening twilight and at night, bombing its targets with smaller numbers of aircraft. Crews carried out parallel day and night reconnaissance flights.

The division successfully bombed German tanks around Kalinovka (a centre of resistance in Pervomaysk) and a command post and warehouse full of fuel and oil on the outskirts of Kuteynikovo. By the end of June 270th BAD, having flown 312 sorties, had lost five 'Peshkas'.

During a rare lull in the fighting during the early summer of 1943, two regiments in Col G A Chuchev's division were trained to perform dive-bombing missions with a flight of Pe-2s. By alternating between dive-bombing and level bombing during operational sorties, they made it difficult for German anti-aircraft gunners to aim accurately. Dive-bombing also led to a higher degree of accuracy for 270th BAD crews.

At the end of summer operations the commander of the Workers' and Peasants' Red Army Air Force, Marshal of Aviation A A Novikov, in analysing combat operations by units and formations equipped with 'Peshkas', noted that the majority 'Lack confidence in applying the dive-bombing method and do not use it sufficiently, and this reduces the bombing effectiveness. They do not use the tactical performance characteristics of the Pe-2 aircraft fully. It is only the commanders of 86th and 240th SBAPs who have persistently trained crews in how to carry out dive-bombing singly and as part of a group, using it in each combat sortie in suitable weather conditions.'

86th SBAP, commanded by Maj F D Beliy, was especially successful during this period. Between 17 July and 6 August 1943 the regiment used dive-bombing in two-thirds of its attacks, inflicting considerable damage on the enemy's railway transport network. Of the 23 regimental-strength missions made by the division, 12 were assessed as 'excellent' by the upper leadership. In the process of carrying out bombing raids more successful tactical procedures were developed. The optimum dive-angles onto the target were defined, as well as the best ways to provide cover for the bombers. As an expression of his gratitude to 270th BAD's leadership cadre, Marshal of Aviation Novikov awarded engraved watches to seven of the best pilots in the division.

On 23 October 1943 270th BAD was transformed into 6th GvBAD, and 86th and 284th SBAPs became 134th and 135th GvBAPs, respectively.

Following the intense battles on the river Molochnaya, in northern Tavriya and in the Donbass, 6th GvBAD experienced a lull in activity. As a result of the summer and autumn Red Army offensive operations in the south during 1943, Germany's 17th Army, which had been deployed to the Crimean peninsula, was cut off. It had only two supply lines remaining – by sea or by air. A decisive assault on the German Crimean defences would have to be carefully planned and would be time consuming. Soviet command ensured a considerable numerical advantage over the enemy, especially in terms of air power.

An offensive by Soviet ground forces began on 8 April 1944, and airmen of 6th GvBAD afforded the tank crews and infantry a great deal of support from the outset. The most intensive fighting for the formation came on 9 April, when it flew 93 sorties (on that day 32 Pe-2s and 12 A-20Bs successfully destroyed the enemy strongpoint at Tomashevka), 18 April (77 sorties) and 23 April (84 sorties). The division lost nine 'Peshkas' during the course of the month, of which four were downed on 15 April alone. These were probably shot down by Bf 109s from I./JG 52.

The liberation of the Crimea and the comprehensive routing of German and Rumanian forces in the region dramatically changed the strategic environment in the southern sector of the Soviet-German Front. With 8th Air Army now finding itself far behind the frontline, Supreme Headquarters decided that all of its units were to be handed over to other air armies. Management of 8th Air Army was in turn transferred to the reserves. Its former commander, Gen T T Khryukin, was posted to a similar position in 1st Air Army, which fought on the 3rd Belarusian Front. 6th GvBAD joined it a short time later.

Following a period of rest and augmentation, the division was to participate in Operation *Bagration* – a general offensive by Soviet forces in Belarussia that was to become one of the largest and most successful campaigns conducted by the Red Army in World War 2. In the first two weeks of the offensive (from 22 June to 5 July 1944) 6th GvBAD flew 431 combat sorties and dropped 319 tonnes (314 tons) of bombs, predominantly from level flight at low altitude because of a persistent low cloud base. During these two weeks, and over the subsequent days of the operation, 6th GvBAD suffered minimal losses (two Pe-2s and two A-20Bs).

The enemy put up greater resistance when attempting to defend East Prussia, with its anti-aircraft artillery proving to be deadlier than fighters by this late stage of the war. For example, in March 1945 seven 'Peshkas' were shot down by ground fire and only six as a result of aerial action. While engaging in active combat with enemy aircraft that

A bomb dropped from a Pe-2 achieves a direct hit on a German ammunition dump

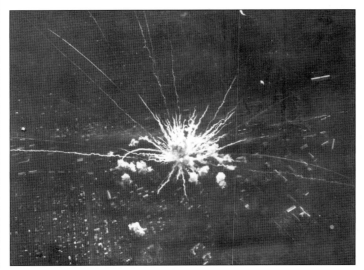

month, 6th GvBAD carried out four raids on the airfield near Pillau during a four-week period. A morning raid by nine dive-bombers on 19 March turned out to be the most successful, with no fewer than five German aircraft being set on fire and the runway and one hangar destroyed. When the unit returned to the airfield a few days later, no enemy fighters were scrambled to intercept them.

Heroes of the Soviet Union A I Balabanov, L N Bobrov, F P Paliy and N I Maykov routinely led combat missions for the division in the last few months of the conflict. Even the younger crews, who were more confident than they had been a year previously, had found their feet in battle and did not lose their composure in critical situations even when targeted by heavy flak. Bombing raids in which five or six groups of nine Pe-2s would participate were commonplace, and had a demoralising effect on the enemy.

4th GvBAP, led by Lt Col Morozov, came under 6th GvBAD control on 24 April 1945 in order to strengthen the division. By the end of April the division had 82 serviceable Pe-2s on strength.

In the weeks following VE Day, the inspection of targets hit by the division confirmed how highly effective the VVS RKKA had been in the concluding phase of the war.

Aircraft from the first Pe-2 squadron of 134th GvBAP, commanded by Maj V M Katkov, prepare to depart on a mission from an airfield in the Crimea during the spring of 1944

Dive-bombers of 134th GvBAP taxi out to takeoff on a bombing mission in the Sevastopol area in the spring of 1944. On 22 April that year the Pe-2 of the regimental commander, Maj Katkov, received a direct hit by a flak shell and made a forced landing in the vicinity of Sapun-gora

GUARDS BOMBER AIR CORPS

Aviation armies began to be formed in the summer of 1942 following a directive from Supreme High Command Headquarters. In contrast to air armies, which were subordinate to the various fronts, aviation armies, according to their founders, were to become a powerful reserve that could be rapidly sent by Supreme High Command Headquarters to augment frontline units in the most important operational areas. The senior Soviet leadership proposed that the application of an aviation army alongside an established air army in a relatively narrow sector of the front would ensure that air supremacy could be won. Securing the latter would be hugely beneficial when it came to assisting ground forces in their struggle against the Wehrmacht.

At first only three aviation army commands were set up – two for fighters (IA, *Istrebitel'naya Armiya* – Fighter Aviation Army) and one for bombers (BA, *Bombardirovochnaya Armiya* – Bomber Aviation Army). Owing to a shortage of trained reservists, the sonorous sounding name of the latter did not fully correspond to the initial plan. To begin with, only two divisions (284th and 285th BADs) became part of 1st BA. With a standard complement of 20 aeroplanes per regiment, this army had around 160 Pe-2s at its disposal. Major-General of Aviation V A Sudets set about establishing command of this amalgamation, which had been deployed to Tambov in accordance with a decree from the People's Commissariat for Defence dated 1 July 1942. At the beginning of the war he had commanded a long-range BAK.

1st BA's line-up was reviewed many times because of the terrible events in the south of the Soviet-German Front in the summer of 1942. Several of the most highly trained divisions were 'withdrawn' and sent to the front, and recently formed (and insufficiently trained) formations replaced them. Under instructions from I V Stalin, five divisions came under 1st BA control in August. The first of these was 221st BAD, flying Douglas DB-7 Boston IIIs that had been manufactured for Britain but were supplied to the USSR as a result of so-called 'dual lend-lease' – they were known simply as B-3s or B-IIIs among Soviet airmen. 222nd BAD was equipped with the North American B-25 Mitchell, which was not widely used in the Soviet Union. Finally, 263rd, 285th and 293rd BADs all flew the Pe-2.

August 1942 also saw 1st BA became operationally subordinate to the commander of the Workers' and Peasants' Red Army Air Force, Lieutenant General of Aviation A A Novikov.

Intensive training and the assimilation of equipment continued among 1st BA's formations up to the beginning of autumn 1942. Tactical flying training took place in Podmoskov'ye, the aim of which was to develop skills in handling large formations operating *en masse* in a restricted area.

However, by this time the appeal of an aviation army had waned somewhat in the eyes of the upper Soviet military leadership.

It became clear that operating both an aviation army and an air army side-by-side from the same base in a restricted area meant that manoeuvring around the airfield when taking off and landing had to be done quickly so as to avoid interference by enemy fighters. Keeping such a large number of aircraft, and personnel, supplied with munitions, parts, fuel and food also took some doing, especially when they had to be mobilised rapidly. Finally, the operational capacity of the existing airfields would not be sufficient for two armies. Moreover, unhealthy competition and friction had arisen between the commanders of the two armies.

Supreme Headquarters therefore made a radical decision to reject the aviation armies and form less cumbersome Supreme Headquarters *Reservniy Aviatsionniy Korpus* (Reserve Air Corps), which would supplement the permanent air armies on the various fronts.

2nd GvBAK

In accordance with a decree issued by the People's Commissariat for Defence dated 10 September 1942, 1st BA became 1st BAK of the Supreme Command Headquarters Reserve. 263rd BAD under Col F I Dobysh and 293rd BAD under Col G V Gribakin were retained, and Major General of Aviation V A Sudets was made commander of the formation. By that time all six air regiments (each of the divisions was comprised of three regiments) were fully equipped with Pe-2 dive-bombers.

Crews underwent preliminary training and were 'broken in' by reserve air regiments, amassing in the region of 30 flying hours on the 'Peshkas' on average. Before being sent to the front, each crew would carry out three to five bombing runs in level flight, three to four transit flights and three to five strafing runs against ground targets. It was only the so-called 'cadre' of the air regiments – the commanders and navigators of the aviation units and squadrons, as well as most of the flight commanders – who had combat experience.

Between 17-21 October 1942 1st BAK was redeployed to 3rd Air Army's airfield complex at Goroshchino and Budovo, from where it began to see action on the Kalinin Front. Supporting an offensive by frontline troops, Sudet's crews started by bombing various targets on the battlefield, as well as strongpoints and centres of resistance.

The weather conditions were not favourable for active sorties, particularly towards the end of 1942. By the beginning of 1943 there were 107 serviceable and five unserviceable Pe-2s, as well as one serviceable B-III, in the six air regiments and the two divisional and corps commands, along with 115 combat-capable crews. 1st BAK had flown 1005 combat sorties up to 29 January 1943, when the formation left the Kalinin Front and redeployed to the Volkhov Front. Of those sorties, 388 made use of dive-bombing. Combat losses stood at 35 'Peshkas', of which 15 were shot down by fighters, nine by flak batteries and 11 failed to return for unknown reasons. The corps lost 83 aircrew.

Despite the enemy's fierce resistance, 'Peshka' crews strived to break through to their assigned targets and fulfil their given missions. Typically, each aircraft carried 700 kg (1540 lbs) of aerial bombs, the standard load comprising two FAB-250s and two FAB-100s, all on external racks.

1st BAK's combat debut on the Kalinin Front generally went well, and the following entry appears in the corps records;

'The entire complement received the thanks of the Commander of the Workers' and Peasants' Red Army Air Force. This was in recognition of its well defined military action, the courage and heroism with which it was carried out, excellent flying skills in dogfights with the German invaders and for active support of ground troops fighting to liberate the town of Velikiye Luki.'

Having accepted such a powerful formation as 1st BAK under its instruction, Supreme Headquarters was later to use it to augment the air armies during offensives. 1st BAK's short tenure on the Volkhov Front was characterised by a comparatively high average bomb load for each Pe-2 (188 combat sorties were flown and 183 tonnes (180 tons) of bombs were dropped). This could be explained by the proximity of the targets to the bombers' home base. Losses amounted to seven 'Peshkas', four of which were shot down by ground fire.

1st BAK's subsequent tenure on the Northwestern Front also turned out to be short-lived too, but the formation was to remain on the Voronezh Front (as part of 2nd Air Army, led by Gen S A Krasovskiy) for a long time. At the very beginning of this period the aircrews heard some good news during a transit flight to the Buturlin airfield complex (technical staff were redeployed using railway transport). In a decree by People's Commissar for Defence Stalin dated 18 March 1943, one of the corps' divisions, 263rd BAD, was to become 1st GvBAD in recognition of its successes, and of its frequent distinction in combat.

As previously mentioned, Fedor Dobysh had become commander of the first GvBAP (4th GvBAP) in the VVS RKKA in 1941. Six months later he was already leading Soviet aviation's first Guards division, 1st GvBAD. All the units in the division subsequently became Guards regiments, 46th SBAP being re-designated 80th GvBAP (led by Maj S P Tyurikov), 202nd SBAP becoming 81st GvBAP (led by Lt Col S P Sennikov) and 321st SBAP becoming 82nd GvBAP (led by Maj N A Rybalchenko). This air division was subsequently titled the Kirovograd Red Banner Air Division of the Order of Bogdan Khmelnitskiy, while its regiments became 80th Guards Chenstokhov Red Banner Air Regiment of the Order of Bogdan Khmelnitskiy, 81st Guards Krakov Air Regiment of the Orders of Suvorov and Bogdan Khmelnitskiy and 82nd Guards Berlin Air Regiment of the Orders of Suvorov and Kutuzov.

The exploits of 1st GvBAD became widely known across all fronts, its participation in an operation becoming, to a certain extent, a guarantee of success. Indeed, the division was mentioned many times in decrees issued by the Supreme Commander, in which he expressed his gratitude.

On 26 March 1943 Gen V A Sudets became commander of the 17th Air Army, and Hero of the Soviet Union Col I S Polbin assumed command of 1st BAK. Many of the corps' successes are linked to Polbin, who proved to be a brilliant theorist and practitioner when it came to using the 'Peshka'. He believed that high performance, powerful weaponry and durability of construction had been brought together successfully in this aircraft. At that time (mid-1943) Ivan Polbin, who was already a 100-mission veteran, was actively advocating the virtues of dive-bombing in newspapers and military journals.

Soon after Polbin took over 1st BAK several unit commanders were rotated out of the corps. One such change of leadership saw 81st GvBAP CO Lt Col S P Sennikov replaced by Maj V Ya Gavrilov. A short time later the latter was awarded the 'Gold Star' hero's medal for his deeds in battle on 16 February 1943. On that date Pe-2 construction number 30/7 was fired upon while being flown by Gavrilov. A large-calibre artillery shell damaged a wing and one aileron and the aircraft caught fire and stalled, entering a spin. Gavrilov, however, levelled the bomber off and, switching on the inert-gas system, extinguished the fire in the wing tanks. Pressing on to the target in his badly damaged aircraft, Gavrilov dropped his bombs on enemy artillery positions. On his return journey he was attacked by Bf 109s, but still managed to coax the aircraft across the frontline before making a forced landing in a field.

A group photograph of the future commander of 2nd GvBAK, Ivan Polbin (centre), and the most distinguished pilots and navigators of 150th SBAP (later 35th GvBAP)

As Soviet forces seized German weaponry and stockpiles of ammunition during the course of their winter offensive, a question arose as to how some of this equipment might be used. Having overcome a series of difficulties regarding the peculiarities of German explosives, units from 1st BAK used Luftwaffe SC 250, SD 250 and SD 50 aerial bombs against their former owners for the first time. This experiment proved to be highly successful, and subsequently the intensity with which 'trophy bombs' were used grew steadily, reaching a peak in the spring of 1945.

A lull descended on the central sectors of the Soviet-German Front from March to July 1943. Command made use of this time to introduce young pilots to the formation, refine bombing techniques and prepare aircraft for the coming summer offensives. Their role in the battle for the Kursk Salient – one of the largest engagements of World War 2 – became a serious test for the units and formations in the Workers' and Peasants' Red Army Air Force, including the BAK equipped with 'Peshkas'.

1st BAK under Col I S Polbin fought as part of 2nd Air Army during the defensive phase of the campaign. Between 5-17 July many crews were working under great pressure, flying up to three sorties a day. Summing up the formations' operations on this front at the time, headquarters noted, 'After a relative lull German fighter activity has repeatedly increased, and they have started to put up fierce resistance'. 1st BAK flew 972 combat sorties and dropped 625.5 tonnes (615.5 tons) of bombs during July. According to reports it had destroyed 518 vehicles and 68 tanks, as well as blowing up 16 warehouses. Its own losses were heavy, however, with some 37 Pe-2s being shot down – at least 16 had fallen victim to ground fire.

At the beginning of August the corps was redeployed to the Steppe Front, where it became part of 5th Air Army. Here, the unit was to support ground forces during the advance on Belgorod and Kharkov. On 3 August – the first day of Operation *Commander Rumyantsev* – 1st BAK carried out a massive raid in which four groups of bombers, escorted by 113 La-5s, dropped around 150 tonnes (147 tons) of bombs. The density of the bomb pattern

created by the corps amounted to 17 tonnes (16.7 tons) of ordnance per 1 km (0.6 miles) of front, and the enemy's principal firepower was suppressed as a result. Only one crew failed to return. Taking advantage of this strike, 53rd Army units advanced forward rapidly.

The military action taken by the corps in the days following this raid was almost as effective, and on as large a scale. However, judging by the increasing number of Pe-2s lost by 1st BAK, enemy aviation had been reinforced. It was not just the young airmen who were listed among the dead and those missing without trace, but also the crew of the corps' inspector of flying procedures, Hero of the Soviet Union Col I P Firsov. He was almost certainly shot down on 14 August by German ace Leutnant Friedrich Obleser of III./JG 52.

However, the Germans incurred significant damage as a result of the action by the corps. The 980 combat sorties flown in July were aimed at bombing enemy forces and equipment, and in August 2120 sorties were flown with the same purpose. The intensity with which the Pe-2s were used is evident in the following table;

An anonymous crew of an early-series Pe-2 fitted with an FT navigator's turret check their map before boarding their aircraft. The white outline to the star insignia indicates that this photograph was taken no earlier than the autumn of 1943

Intensity of 1st BAK combat operations July-August 1943

Time period	Number of sorties	Number of flying days	Average number of serviceable aircraft	Number of sorties flown by each Pe-2 per month
July	1051	13	102	10.03
August	2263	23	126	18.0

From the autumn of 1943 dive-bombing began to be used more widely across the bomber divisions and corps, but it was within 1st GvBAD units that the adoption of this method of attack was treated with the greatest degree of responsibility. It became a rule among Polbin's crews to perform three or four dives over their own territory for training purposes while regrouping a formation after an attack. This in turn caused the commander of the corps to issue a decree stating that this element of training should only be performed by those pilots whose aircraft have not been damaged by fire from enemy fighters or artillery during the course of the sortie.

By late autumn 1943 1st BAK was considered fully prepared for dive-bombing operations and the sphere of missions carried out by the Pe-2s expanded. Railway stations, which were used intensively by the enemy, increasingly came under attack. For example, on 28 November all three bomber regiments, led by Capts V P Shishkin and N V Ogurtsov, bombed Znamenka station from level flight. Sixty FAB-100 and FAB-250 bombs were dropped and up to 15 vehicles were destroyed. Steam locomotives and railway tracks were also destroyed, which interrupted movements through Znamenka for four days. The unit that enjoyed the most success during the course of the mission was 81st GvBAP, led on this occasion by Snr Lt P Ya Gusenko. Almost all of the bombs dropped by its aeroplanes hit the target.

A line-up of crews from 161st GvBAP in mid 1944. Note the white vertical stripe on the rear fuselage and the tactical numbers on the fin of the Pe-2 closest to the camera, comprising both the aircraft's number in the regiment and the squadron number

The new year brought unseasonably warm weather, low cloud and frequent fog in the Ukraine. Nevertheless, Soviet aviation continued to take the fight to the enemy, participating in the Kirovograd and Korsun-Shevchenkov offensives. Both were successful, the enemy being routed and demoralised.

On 5 February the regiments within 1st BAK were transformed by a decree from the Supreme Commander in recognition of their determination, distinction in combat and the collective heroism shown by personnel in the battle for the Kursk Salient and the right bank of the Ukraine. 1st BAK became 2nd GvBAK, 293rd BAD became 8th GvBAD and 780th, 804th and 854th BAPs became 160th, 161st and 162nd GvBAPs (the commanders of these air regiments were Lt Col F D Lushchayev, Maj A M Semenov and Lt Col L A Novikov, respectively).

By that time enough information had been assembled to allow the positive and negative aspects of the Pe-2 from an operational perspective to be assessed. The general conclusion was that 'the Pe-2 fully meets the requirements asked of a dive-bomber'. During this same period, claims of insufficient firepower in the aircraft's aft hemisphere were expressed. It was noted that it was absolutely impossible to beat off attacks by fighters in a dive as the VK-105PF engines were comparatively low-powered and did not correspond to the aircraft's flying weight. The lack of a mechanism for retracting the airbrake grids in an emergency proved disastrous for many crews, as the aircraft's speed was reduced to 240-260 km/h (150-160 mph) when extended, making the Pe-2 a sitting duck for enemy fighters.

During the second half of 1944 the 'closed circle' combat formation was widely used during raids. In this case each crew would make several dive-bombing runs on the target,

Maj Zvontsov leads a flight of Pe-2s from 854th BAP on a combat mission during 1943. Gunners/radio operators observe the rear hemispheres. Note the MV-2 hatch turrets with UBT machine guns in their firing positions on the aircraft trailing Zvontsov's Pe-2

Col Fedor Dobysh, commander of 4th GvBAP, which was part of 1st BAK. This photograph provides a more complete view of the crocodile nose art seen on the Pe-2 occasionally flown by Dobysh

Bottom left
Col Ivan Polbin was commander of 1st BAK, which was later re-formed as 2nd GvBAK

Bottom right
This diagram depicts a dive-bombing attack using the 'Polbin rotation'. The idea was to close up the formation to such an extent that the trailing aircraft covered the tail of the one in front, both in normal flight and when diving and pulling out. During this manoeuvre each approach to the target was made from a different direction, making it difficult for the enemy to organise an effective defence

which increased accuracy. One of the founders of this attack method, Gen Polbin tested its effectiveness himself during the Lvov-Sandomir operation. On 15 July he led 15 Pe-2s on a raid to strike a concentration of enemy tanks and artillery positions close to the Beliy Kamen settlement, and a second group of ten aircraft was led by Col F I Dobysh.

The aircraft entered a dive from an altitude of 1200 metres (4000 ft) and levelled out at 350 metres (1150 ft). While the first aircraft carried out its attack, a second was on approach to the target and a third and fourth were preparing to start their bombing runs. The fifth aircraft out of the five closed the circle. According to reports from crews, 180 vehicles, nine tanks, up to 40 carts and an artillery battery were destroyed, and many troops were killed. The raid was repeated the following day.

During the Lvov-Sandomir operation Soviet dive-bombers used the 'closed circle' tactic many times without losing a single bomber. When employed correctly, the tactic proved to be a challenging one for German flak gunners to deal with, as the speed, heading and altitude of the aircraft in the circle constantly changed, making aiming difficult. As a rule, 88 mm artillery rounds would explode some distance from the outside of the circle, and not one explosion was recorded inside the circle in July 1944.

The average time for a bombing run on the enemy in a Pe-2 had been one to two minutes, but with the adoption of the 'closed circle' tactic this had now increased to up to 15-20 minutes. According to the testimony of German prisoners of war, Wehrmacht forces were demoralised by these raids.

In a further change to the tactics being employed by Pe-2 units, on the initiative of 2nd GvBAK's commander, approaches to the target would in future be made from multiple directions. This new method was called the 'Polbin rotation' after its founder.

In the concluding phase of the war 2nd GvBAK, which had been awarded the honorary title of 'Lvov' in late 1944, participated in all of the offensives on the 1st Ukrainian Front, including the Vislo-Silez campaign, which took place between 11 January and 1 March 1945. The corps was under 2nd Air Army control during this period, and it had 193 combat aircraft on strength on the eve of the offensive.

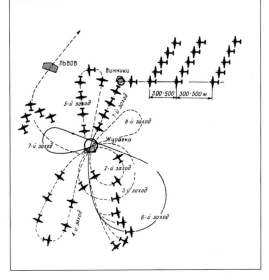

2nd GvBAK suffered a number of casualties during the Vislo-Silez campaign, one of whom was its commanding officer. The following entry appears in the corps' historical record of service;

'On 11 February 1945 the commander of the Guards Corps, Maj Gen Ivan Semyonovich Polbin, was killed during a raid on the area around the town of Breslau.'

The commander of the 1st Ukrainian Front, Marshal I S Konev, described his subordinate as follows;

'Twice Hero of the Soviet Union Gen Polbin, commander of 2nd GvBAK, was an extremely brave man. It was this personal bravery that suited his organisational and command qualities well. He continued to fly combat sorties throughout the war, particularly if they were large in scale, crucial to the war effort or particularly dangerous in nature.'

Following Polbin's death the corps was taken on and led to victory by Col (soon to become Maj Gen) D T Nikishin. He led a large group of 74 Pe-2s on a daylight raid on 5 May to strike enemy troops and equipment close to Breslau. As a result of this powerful air raid the fortress garrison ceased to offer any resistance.

Twice Hero of the Soviet Union Capt Pavel A Plotnikov, who had flown the Pe-2 since the beginning of the war, was one of the more decorated pilots to serve with 2nd GvBAK. By May 1944, when Plotnikov was first recommended for the country's highest award, he had 225 combat sorties to his credit. He and his crew had also shot down three enemy aircraft. Made commander of 81st GvBAP in the autumn of that year, Plotnikov flew a total of 344 combat sorties – around half of them saw him using the Pe-2 as a dive-bomber. He was particularly prolific in 1944-45, when he sank six transport vessels, blew up six trains and destroyed three railway bridges.

Plotnikov's regimental colleague, Capt Nikolai Gapeenok, had flown 223 sorties by war's end (he flew the Pe-2 as a dive-bomber in 125 of them). The brave and decisive actions of his crew were mentioned many times in memoranda concerning 1st GvBAD and 2nd GvBAK. Capt Pavel Gusenko, another of 81st GvBAP's dive-bombing aces, became known for the sniper-like accuracy of his attacks. This courageous pilot was not destined to see victory, however, for he was killed over Presov station on 20 September 1944 during his 196th combat sortie.

Hero of the Soviet Union Capt Pavel Plotnikov (left) with his navigator, Capt Konstantin Mulyukin, of 81st GvBAP. Plotnikov later became the second aviator in the corps after deceased corps commander Polbin to be twice awarded with the title of Hero of the Soviet Union. A pre-war Pe-2 pilot, Plotnikov flew 303 combat sorties and survived the conflict

Pe-2 construction number 14/136, flown by pilot Ekaterina Fedotova, navigator Klara Dubkova and radio-operator/gunner Antonina Khokhlova of 125th GvBAP, had a swallow painted on its nose. This veteran crew had flown 14/136 throughout its time in the frontline

1st GvBAK

The history of the formation of 1st GvBAK is in many ways similar to that of 2nd GvBAK. The corps was formed as 2nd BAK between 10 October and 20 November 1942 by Maj Gen I L Turkel. Initially it was only 221st and 285th BADs (the latter consisting of Pe-2-equipped 134th and 205th SBAPs and 35th GvBAP) under the command of Hero of the Soviet Union V A Sandalov that became part of the new formation. By late November, however, Turkel had replaced 221st BAD (which flew Boston IIIs) with 223rd BAD (comprised of Pe-2-equipped 10th, 99th and 224th BAPs) under Lt Col L N Yuzeyev.

There was an acute shortage of crews trained to fly the Pe-2 in combat in late 1942. For example, there was not a single aviator in 10th Red Banner SBAP who had previously seen action in the type. And while the general flying skills of pilots in the corps were acknowledged to be good, they were not given any training in dive-bombing. Indeed, only 134th SBAP ensured that its crews were taught individual flying and level-flight bombing techniques for the Pe-2 in good weather conditions. In fact the regiment had 17 crews that had previously flown 'Peshkas' in the frontline, with some having completed as many as 60 combat sorties.

Meanwhile, important events were brewing on the southern flank of the Soviet-German Front. The Red Army had launched a counterattack outside Stalingrad, and on 20 November 1942 2nd BAK left for the Don Front to augment 16th Air Army. It was here that the process of refinement of training continued. 134th SBAP, which was considered to be the corps' best-trained regiment, went into action on 10 December, while the other five followed suit some time later. According to a report, 2nd BAK had flown 305 combat sorties up to 19 December, predominantly in bad weather, bombing area targets and airfields, carrying out reconnaissance and hitting separate, pinpoint targets. Crews also flew 60 sorties at night.

At the start of the fighting the corps had 126 Pe-2s, and during the early weeks of the campaign it lost ten aircraft, predominantly to enemy fighters. Eight Pe-2s were also damaged by flak and had to make emergency landings. Most of these machines were soon repaired thanks to the efforts of regimental technical staff. Gen Turkel noted that in December 1942 there had been one unrecoverable loss for every 30 combat sorties, which was testimony to the enemy's fierce resistance. Nevertheless, at that time this figure seemed considerably better than the high sortie-to-loss ratio that had been a grim feature of the defensive battles outside Stalingrad.

By the end of 1942 a seventh regiment in the form of 587th Women's SBAP had become part of 2nd BAK. The formation of women's air regiments in the USSR is linked first and foremost with the name of Marina Raskova, Hero of the Soviet Union and someone who participated in many record-breaking long-distance flights as a member of all-women crews between 1935-38.

In October 1941 Raskova approached Stalin with a suggestion to form a women's air group made up of volunteer women pilots who had previously worked as instructors at aero clubs, flying schools and on Civilian Air Fleet routes. Given the designation 122, the group was later transformed into three regiments – a fighter regiment flying Yak-1s, one for light night bombers flying U-2s and one for daylight bombers flying the Su-2. Raskova herself decided to lead the last of these, but she felt that the Su-2 was not fast or modern enough to perform the mission effectively – by then production had already ceased. Using her direct links with Stalin, Marina Raskova succeeded in re-equipping the regiment with Pe-2s.

For all its advantages over the single-engined, obsolescent, Su-2 and the equally venerable twin-engined SB, the 'Peshka' distinguished itself only in terms of its speed. The bomber could not fly on one engine without losing altitude, and it placed high demands on the flying skills of the pilot when landing. Only strong aviators loved it, with weak pilots being somewhat afraid of it. With this firmly in mind, only female pilots who exhibited such attributes would receive training to fly the Pe-2. Their conversion was carried out at the Engels Flying School, with Capt E D Timofeyeva being the first to complete a solo flight in a Pe-2 on 4 August 1942. Four months later 587th SBAP transferred to Kirzhach airfield, where a temporary base had been set up. On 4 January 1943 the aircraft flown by Maj Marina Raskova crashed in bad weather and the crew was killed.

587th SBAP, which was given the name of Maj Raskova, was then taken over by Maj V V Markov, who was to remain in this post until war's end. The posts of his subordinates, his deputy (Capt Yevgeniya Timofeyeva), chief of staff (Capt Militsa Kazarinova), regimental navigator (Capt Valentina Kravchenko) and other positions were held by women at that time. Markov subsequently recalled;

'I cannot say that my first experience of commanding this regiment was easy for me. Up until that time no woman had ever flown a dive-bomber. Doubts naturally crept in. How would the girls cope with such a difficult task in combat conditions? However, these worries proved to be unfounded.'

In Soviet history the air battle over the Kuban is seen as an important step towards air supremacy along the entire Soviet-German Front. In planning the air offensive, Supreme Headquarters trained and drafted in huge reserves for the battle, including 2nd BAK, ensuring a considerable numerical advantage over the Luftwaffe. The corps fought as part of 4th Air Army on the Northwestern Front.

On the evening of 28 April units from 2nd BAK took part in the first strike against the enemy when two groups of nine 'Peshkas' were despatched. Subsequently, even larger mass raids were performed using Pe-2s, attacking pockets of resistance at Krymsk, Moldavska and Verkhniy Agadun railway stations, among others. Up to 6 June 1943 2nd BAK had flown 1328 combat sorties and dropped 903 tonnes (888 tons) of bombs, losing 39 'Peshkas', of which four were non-combat losses.

Changes took place in 2nd BAK's line-up during the course of the events described above, and before the battle of Kursk. In February 1943 Gen V A Ushakov had become commander of the corps, replacing Gen Turkel, who was made the chief inspector of the Workers' and Peasants' Red Army Air Force. Col A M Smirnov became chief of staff in May and F P Kotlyar was given command of 223rd BAD. It was likely that the division was also put

On 2 July 1942 Mariya Dolina's Pe-2 was attacked by Bf 109s and both engines were set on fire, but she managed to crash-land the bomber in a forest clearing and all of the crew escaped unscathed. Subsequently made a deputy squadron commander in 125th GvBAP, Dolina was awarded the title of Hero of the Soviet Union on 18 August 1945 for completing 72 successful combat missions

The crew of pilot Lt Irina Osadze (centre), navigator Lyudmila Popova (left) and radio-operator/gunner Taisiya Panferova (right) also served with 125th GvBAP

in charge of the 'extraordinary' 99th and 3rd BAPs at this time so that the 223rd could retain its three-regiment structure.

2nd BAK did not participate in the defence of Kursk, the corps instead coming under 15th Air Army control on the Bryansk Front during the counterattack on the Orlovsk salient. Although the fighting was limited to just two days in July 1943, a group sortie on the 14th led to the loss of seven Pe-2s of the 18 involved.

Capt Nadezhda Fedutenko (left), who was a squadron CO in 125th GvBAP, was later made a Hero of the Soviet Union. Before joining the Pe-2 regiment she had completed 200+ combat sorties in the R-5. Fedutenko flew 56 combat missions in the Pe-2

Corps operations on the Western Front in August as part of 1st Air Army were more successful, although the sorties took place amid fierce fighting. In the space of a month 53 aircraft were holed by flak, not counting those damaged by Bf 109s and Fw 190s.

The following statistics detail the role of 1st and 2nd BAKs in the battle for the Kursk Salient in the period from 5 July to 23 August 1943;

1st and 2nd BAK Combat Line-up between July and August 1943

Formation	On hand beginning month	Overall losses	Number of combat losses	New arrivals	On hand at end of month	Time period
1st BAK	179 Pe-2s	52	40	29	156 Pe-2s	July 1943
2nd BAK	122 Pe-2s	30	8	26	118 Pe-2s	July 1943
1st BAK	160 Pe-2s	59	50	44	145 Pe-2s	August 1943
2nd BAK	118 Pe-2s	20	17	16	114 Pe-2s	August 1943

Statistics for Pe-2 Losses

Formation	Number of sorties	Losses	Losses to fighters	Losses to flak	Failed to return	Time period
1st BAK	1051	36	21	-	15	July
2nd BAK	67	8	7	-	1	July
1st BAK	2263	45	17	21	7	August
2nd BAK	1140	17	5	7	5	August

In a decree issued by the People's Commissariat for Defence, dated 3 September 1943, 2nd BAK became 1st GvBAK, and 223rd and 285th BADs were re-designated 4th and 5th GvBADs, respectively. Five of the regiments in the corps then became Guards regiments, being designated 124th to 128th GvBAPs.

Following a pause in operations, the corps continued to participate in the Smolensk offensive as part of 1st Air Army, assisting ground troops on the Western Front to break through the strongly reinforced enemy defences.

Amid the successful combat sorties, there were occasions when missions did not go to plan. For example, on 12 October 1943 the commander of 4th GvBAD ordered that his crews were to strike artillery and mortar positions, as well as concentrations of troops, around Lyudinichi, Zastenok

The devastating results of a bombing attack by Pe-2s on a German motorised column

and Kozlovshchina, using four groups of nine aircraft. The group was to be escorted by 18 fighters from 309th IAD. Lt Cols Prokofyev and Zhivolup, who had been sent ahead to rendezvous with the fighter units, were unable to land at 309th IAD's airfield owing to fog. At the appointed time 36 Pe-2s led by divisional commander Col F P Kotlyar approached the fighters' airfield, but the escort failed to take off despite four circuits being made overhead by the 'Peshkas'.

It was 32 minutes before the Yaks took off, but initially the plan was for them to escort 5th GvBAD, not the 4th! As a result the leader lost his orientation owing to nervousness and the long wait and ended up dropping his bombs on his own territory. Luckily nobody was hurt. Three other groups of nine bombers did not drop their bombs at all, returning to base with their loads intact.

The pilots of the French Normandie Regiment, which became part of 303rd IAD, would often escort the women's regiment. During one such mission, they took a difficult route from Russia's Central regions to Eastern Prussia, fighting in the skies over Yelnya, Smolensk, Borisov and other towns. Recognising that the Pe-2 was 'far from being a woman's aeroplane', the French fighter pilots expressed their admiration for the unprecedented levels of courage exhibited by the Soviet aviators. In one of the messages addressed to the women's regiment after the war, French ace and Hero of the Soviet Union Jacques Andre wrote;

'I greet my comrades in arms, the young Soviet women pilots who did not concede to the men at all in their courage during the battles against our common enemy, as sisters.'

Following an extended period of rest and re-equipment (from 1 January to 21 June 1944), during which time 1st GvBAK's units were engaged in various forms of combat training, the corps returned to action once again when it became part of 1st Air Army. At that point 40 Heroes of the Soviet Union were serving in 1st GvBAK, which by then had been awarded the honorary title of 'Vitebsk' for its successes in combat. The corps flew 1207 combat sorties, dropping 874 tonnes (860 tons) of bombs in the period from 22 June (the start of Operation *Bagration*) to 12 July 1944. Attacks on enemy airfields in the 3rd Belarusian Front's sector became frequent, and according to reports from crews 45 German aircraft were destroyed by 1st GvBAK, predominantly on the ground.

Although the Red Army had struck with such colossal force in the initial phase of Operation *Bagration* that the enemy was literally shocked into submission in Belarussia, in the Baltic region, where Ushakov's 1st GvBAK would later see action, the balance of forces turned out to be less favourable. From 23 July 1944 to 8 February 1945 1st GvBAK's bombers flew 4073 combat sorties and dropped 3562 tonnes (3505 tons) of bombs. The following statistics testify to the intensity of the campaign in the Baltic. Combat losses amounted to 86 Pe-2s, predominantly from attacks by enemy fighters from JG 54 'Green Hearts'. Non-combat losses amounted to 12 aircraft. According to reports from crews, 83 enemy aircraft were destroyed in the air and a further 52 on their airfields.

In the majority of cases the crews of the Pe-2s carried out their missions successfully, given reliable fighter cover. There were, however, exceptions, when sorties would end in a substantial loss of life. Such was the case on 14 September 1944 during a raid on an enemy airfield in the centre of Riga. Three groups of 'Peshkas' encountered anti-aircraft fire en route, and this grew in intensity the closer the Pe-2s got to the city. Crews reported that 400 rounds could be seen exploding simultaneously at an altitude of 4500 metres (14,700 ft). Despite an escort of 38 P-39 Airacobras, some 20 Fw 190s broke through to the bombers and shot six of them down. 124th GvBAP CO Lt Col G A Nikolayev and his crew were killed, whilst the crew of squadron leader Capt N G Borisov from the same unit was taken prisoner.

In all 124th BAP lost no fewer than 11 'Peshkas' during the course of the mission. According to German records, the Fw 190s were from I./JG 54, which reported 13 Pe-2s shot down. High-scoring ace Oberleutnant Franz Eisenach, who led the Fw 190s in their attack on the bombers, was credited with four Pe-2s destroyed – he also claimed five Il-2s that same day.

At the end of June 1944 Gen Ushakov's 1st GvBAK became 5th GvBAK in order to 'avoid numerical duplication as Long Range Aviation merges with the Air Force'. In this period most of the Pe-2 units in the corps rarely resorted to dive-bombing, preferring to drop their bombs from low or medium altitudes and in level flight. It was only individual crews that perfected the tactic of dive-bombing. Others sought to load the aircraft with the maximum payload of bombs, and achieved remarkable successes. For example, in April 1945 the average payload for a 'Peshka' bombing targets in Eastern Prussia, the fortresses and ports of Konigsberg and Pillau, as well as other locations, was 906 kg (2000 lbs) during very intense military action. Some crews, however, took this up to 1200 kg (2645 lbs), which would have been considered both inconceivable and dangerous in 1942-43. The corps ended the war as part of 13th Air Army on the Leningrad Front.

GUARDS RECONNAISSANCE AIR REGIMENTS

A directive from the chief of Red Army General Headquarters (GK KA, *Glavnoe Komandovanie Krasnoy Armii*), dated 21 July 1942, stated 'a 2nd Reconnaissance Air Regiment of Red Army General Headquarters is to be formed to fly the reconnaissance versions of the Pe-2 aircraft, and is to be deployed to Monino'. Order No 1, concerning the formation of the regiment, was signed by its first commander, Maj V M Chuvilo, on 1 August 1941. 2nd RAP (*Razvedyvatel'nyy Aviatsionniy Polk* – Reconnaissance Air Regiment) had 25 Pe-2s and 17 crews who had undergone conversion during June-July 1941. However, it was unable to take up combat duties immediately because the overwhelming majority of its personnel had no experience of reconnaissance flying, and the pilots and navigators augmenting the regiment were not trained on the Pe-2 at all.

The regiment's first combat sortie was undertaken on 3 October 1941 by 2Lts Alyshev and Roslyakov. From 8 October the former commander of 314th RAP, T R Tyurin, took command of the regiment, remaining in this post to war's end. During October-November 1941 the regiment carried out reconnaissance on an enemy force advancing towards Moscow, crews flying 117 combat sorties and often recording areas where enemy forces were concentrated. During the counterattack by Red Army units directly west of Moscow in December 1941, the regiment's crews carried out photo-reconnaissance of the enemy's defensive positions, their network of airfields and operational reserves.

2nd RAP's crews flew 398 combat sorties in the winter of 1941-42, and by 1 January 1942 it had lost 16 aircraft and 48 aircrew.

2nd RAP was also one of the first regiments in the VVS RKKA to receive the Tu-2 for assessment. Five of its more experienced crews, led

A group photograph of aircrew from the second squadron of 2nd RAP, taken in the summer of 1942. Some of these men had previously served with the 'Monino squadron', which formed the core of 2nd RAP upon its formation on 1 August 1941

A Pe-2 reconnaissance aeroplane of 2nd RAP is prepared for its next sortie. This is an early-series aircraft with a glazed nose. This regiment, formed by Maj Vasiliy Chuvilo, also flew a handful of DB-3Fs and Pe-3s alongside the Pe-2, 26 of which formed the backbone of the unit. The cigar-shaped external fuel tanks under the fuselage were a characteristic feature of the photo-reconnaissance Pe-2

The crew of flight commander Capt Romanov (centre) of 2nd RAP. On several occasions this pilot brought his aircraft home after it had been heavily damaged by enemy fighters or flak

by squadron commander Rudevich, departed for Factory No 166 in Omsk in May 1942. On 30 October 1942 a group of four of the new Tu-2 bombers touched down at the regiment's base in Monino. 2nd RAP itself adapted the aircraft into a reconnaissance platform, just as it had done with the Pe-2.

In the summer of 1942 one operational group from 2nd RAP saw action over Stalingrad, while another was sent to the Kalinin Front during an offensive operation by Soviet forces around Rzhev. In early autumn a group of nine day and four night crews were deployed to Migalovo airfield, and from there they carried out aerial reconnaissance of the interior up to Riga, Minsk and Konotop until the end of December, when all of the regiment's crews returned to Monino from their forward airfields.

During the course of a year of intensive fighting the regiment had flown 1341 combat sorties, amassing 3002 flying hours. A total of 82 airfields had been reconnoitered and 140 large settlements and 351 railway junctions surveyed. Losses amounted to 32 aircraft and 75 personnel in 1942. As of 31 December 1942 the regiment had 24 combat-capable aircraft and 32 crews at its disposal. In a year the regiment had received 26 Pe-2s, six Pe-3s, five DB-3Fs and four Tu-2s.

On 26 December 1942 the head of the reconnaissance department of the Workers' and Peasants' Red Army Air Force, Major-General of Aviation D D Grendal, approached Air Force command with a proposal to transform 2nd RAP of GK KA into 1st Guards Air Reconnaissance Regiment of General Headquarters (GvRAP of GK KA). His proposal was favourably received, but the special numbering for the Guards reconnaissance regiment was turned down. An order from the People's Commissariat for Defence, dated 8 February 1943, stated that 2nd RAP of GK KA had been transformed into 47th GvRAP of GK KA 'in recognition of the courage, determination and organisation, as well as the heroism demonstrated by its personnel in battle against the German invaders'.

In the spring and summer of 1943 the regiment supported preparations for two Red Army offensive operations simultaneously, namely the Smolensk-Roslavl and the Orel-Bryansk.

In 1944 the regiment undertook combat operations using a six-squadron format, consisting of 46 aircraft and 42 day and 17 night crews. The Pe-2 was in service with the third and fourth squadrons, with the first squadron flying Tu-2s, the second Il-4s and the fifth Lisunov Li-2s. The sixth squadron was a dedicated training unit equipped with Pe-2 and UPe-2 aircraft. In February 1944 the entire first squadron was posted to a new division that was being formed to fly the Tu-2. The replacement first squadron was re-equipped with 'Peshkas'.

Between January and March 1944, 47th GvRAP carried out reconnaissance concerned with lifting the siege of Leningrad. In June it supplied essential information to general headquarters and the commanders of the Leningrad Front during the breaching of the

Mannerheim Line and the liberation of the fortress city of Vyborg. During June-August 1944 reconnaissance aircraft from the regiment were instrumental in providing critical intelligence for Red Army formations that routed German forces in sectors on the 1st Baltic and the 1st, 2nd and 3rd Belarusian Fronts.

47th GvRAP also played a key role in the preparations for Operation *Bagration*. By the start of the Red Army's offensive, Luftwaffe fighter bases at Orsha, Ulla, Polotsk, Minsk, Baranovichi, Bialystok, Borisov, Mogilev, Lida and other locations had been photographed. With *Bagration* in full swing, the cameras of 47th GvRAP's Pe-2s captured the enemy's all-out retreat, which at times broke into a flight. This entry in the regimental diary reveals the scale of the rout;

'On 26 June 1944 Shishkin's crew came across a column of 1670 vehicles and carts on the move, Lt Petrov came across a column of 1800 units moving west, while Lt Shmut observed a column of 2900 units and a column of 3000 vehicles and carts on 28 June. Lt Ryzhkov observed a column of 1380 units, and one consisting of 6000 vehicles and carts on 29 June. Lt Zhernovoy came across a column of 2300 vehicles and carts.'

From July 1944 the entire regiment was based at Smolensk airfield. During that month 47th GvRAP was awarded 'the honorary name of "Borisov" for its exemplary execution of orders from command when fighting German invaders during the crossing of the river Berezina, and for the liberation of the city of Borisov'. In addition, the regiment was awarded the Order of the Red Banner.

Crews from 47th GvRAP flew 1482 combat sorties, 2721 training flights and 1048 miscellaneous flights during 1944. That year its personnel were awarded 527 government awards, and on 4 February 1944 Guards Capts A F Popov, E L Melakh and R L Yashchuk were the first in the regiment to be awarded the title of Hero of the Soviet Union. Losses in 1944 amounted to 42 aircraft, 17 crews and 79 personnel. As of 1 January 1945 the regiment had 25 Pe-2s, two Tu-2s, two B-25s and seven Il-4s on strength.

From January to May 1945 the regiment provided aerial reconnaissance for the encirclement and routing of enemy troops defending East Prussia and Szczecin. Between December 1944 and January 1945, while operating from airfields in Poland (Krynki, Bel and Modlin), crews flew 446 combat sorties, carrying out reconnaissance on 55 airfields, 126 large railway junctions and 148 cities and large population centres. During one such mission in early January, Guards Senior Lt Dunayevskiy's crew took detailed aerial photographs of the city of Berlin from an altitude of 7000 metres (23,000 ft) in response to an order issued by Supreme Command Headquarters. The regiment was awarded the Order of Suvorov III Class in a decree from the Supreme Soviet of the USSR following this operation.

The crew of a later-series reconnaissance Pe-2 prepare for their next sortie. Note the open hatch in the underside of the fuselage to allow the pilot and navigator to gain access to the cockpit, and the two apertures for camera lenses behind it, the latter equipment filling the bomb-bay

During April-May 1945 the regiment's crews flew 1305 combat sorties, in the course of which 54 cities, 69 railway junctions, 77 airfields and 21 harbours were surveyed. On 23 April the regiment incurred its final loss of the Great Patriotic War when section commander Guards Snr Lt Dunayevskiy's crew failed to return from a sortie to survey Berlin. Considered to be the best crew in the regiment, Dunayevskiy and his men had flown 106 combat sorties since April 1944. They had been attacked by fighters on 13 occasions and fired upon by flak 48 times. The rolls of film exposed by the crew recorded images of 148 airfields housing 2679 aircraft, around 32,000 vehicles, 3436 trains, 325 tanks and 925 ships and vessels. While they were still alive Dunayevskiy and his navigator, Nurpisov, were recommended for the title of Hero of the Soviet Union, but the awards were made posthumously.

During the Great Patriotic War 47th GvRAP flew 4463 combat sorties, amassing 9810 flying hours. A total of 19,646 cities and large population centres, 16,836 railway junctions and stations and 4469 airfields were surveyed. The regiment lost 297 personnel, 83 crews and 99 aircraft. On 9 May 1945 there were 46 crews in the regiment, seven flying the Tu-2, ten the Il-4, 27 the Pe-2 and two the B-25.

48th GvRAP

On 22 June 1941 40th SBAP, based on the airfield at Vindava, in Latvia, had 54 SBs on strength as part of 6th SAD. By then ten of the regiment's pilots, including CO Maj I E Mogilniy, had undergone conversion onto the Pe-2. However, the regiment did not have any aircraft of this type at its disposal.

At 0407 hrs on 22 June Vindava was attacked by 12 German aircraft, which bombed and strafed the hard-standings. More than a dozen SBs were set on fire or damaged. The following morning 40th SBAP's senior engineer reported that only 22 serviceable aircraft remained – a further 14 had made emergency landings. Nevertheless, on 29 June a group of SBs attacked and successfully destroyed the Krustpils bridge, and three days later another enemy crossing point was eliminated across the Zapadnaya Dvina. By the time the regiment's first 'frontline tour' of the war had come to an end on 15 July 1941, it had flown more than 300 combat sorties (some at night). The handful of surviving SBs were passed on to another unit and the regiment withdrew to re-form.

Having arrived at Novocherkassk by 22 July, 40th SBAP set about converting to the Pe-3 heavy fighter – the two-seat variant of the Pe-2, with increased range and slightly improved weaponry. Having completed its training, the regiment headed to Ramenskoye on 30 August to receive its new equipment. 40th SBAP then moved to Serpukhov to commence combat operations with the 32 Pe-3s it had been issued with. Capt I F Lavrentsov became the regiment's commander, replacing Maj Mogilniy who had been killed in a flying accident during the conversion phase.

From 22 to 24 September 1941 the regiment made a series of massive raids on the railway junction at Staraya Russa, putting it out of action for a week. On 27 and 28 September 16 Pe-3s in groups led by Capts Rogov and Malofeyev bombed the railway station at Roslavl and brought train movements to a stop for two to three days. The regiment's losses for September amounted to four Pe-3s, of which two were non-combat related.

During October and November 40th SBAP repeatedly attacked the bridges spanning the river Urga, and also damaged a bridge across the Volga near Kalinin. Losses in October amounted to 13 aircraft, some of which were newly-delivered Pe-2s. The fierce resistance offered by enemy fighters at this time resulted in four Pe-3s being shot down by Bf 109s, while a further six failed to return from their combat sorties for unknown reasons. One of the crews to be killed was that of squadron commander Capt A G Rogov on 8 October. According to a report by I V Malay, who served as a wingman to Rogov, the latter's 'Peshka' was hit by anti-aircraft fire, burst into flames and smashed into a railway bridge across the River Urga.

By the time of his demise, Rogov had flown 60 combat sorties. This effort had earned him a recommendation for the title of Hero of the Soviet Union. The order by which he was to be awarded the USSR's highest honour was dated 22 October 1941.

In all, the regiment flew 365 combat sorties during the defence of Moscow, dropping 218 tonnes (214 tons) of bombs. Between 4 and 14 December 40th SBAP was transferred to 6th IAK. It was then transformed into an aviation reconnaissance regiment assigned to General Headquarters. At that time 40th RAP was equipped with four Pe-2s and eight Pe-3s, which were based at Monino. Soon after the unit changed its mission the CO, Capt Lavrentsov, suffered serious injuries following an aborted takeoff in a Pe-2 from Monino. His place was taken by Maj P M Sadov.

In the spring of 1942 the regiment operated in small operational groups in the most important sectors of the Soviet-German Front. Aircraft of 40th RAP carried out reconnaissance of the largest German airfields in-theatre, namely Seshcha, Alsufevo, Bryansk and Orel, and followed the enemy's redeployment into the depths of occupied territory. As of 1 May 1942 the regiment had four Pe-3s and five Pe-2s on strength, and that month they were supplemented by five Pe-3bis fitted with 20 mm guns in the forward fuselage section. 40th RAP also received a handful of B-25Cs and Airacobras.

During preparations for the offensive operation at Stalingrad, 40th RAP carried out uninterrupted reconnaissance of enemy defensive positions. In this way it made a significant contribution to the creation of a unified photomap of the whole area, elements of which were sent to Red Army units in the field. The map in its entirety was used by command at the fronts, and also by Supreme Command Headquarters to plan a subsequent counterattack.

As of 20 December 1942 the regiment had ten Pe-2s, ten Pe-3s and three B-25Cs at its disposal.

Following an order from 2nd RAP of GK KA, the regiment was transformed into 48th GvRAP. This change of designation was an acknowledgement of 'successes in battle and for the heroism demonstrated by regimental personnel'.

In January 1944 the regiment received a number of photo-reconnaissance Pe-2s fitted with M-82F radial engines for combat evaluation. It was expected that the outcome of this trial would be positive. Indeed, some of the heads of reconnaissance departments in the Red Army, having familiarised themselves with Experimental Design Bureau 22's 'advertised' information concerning the high-flight performance characteristics of this aircraft, worked very hard to ensure that the radial-engined Pe-2 was introduced quickly into frontline service.

However, in the opinion of the commander of 48th GvRAP, Lt Col P S Lozenko, Pe-2s fitted with M-82F engines proved to be worse than standard 'Peshkas', even though their engines were one-and-a-half times more powerful than the inline M-105s. The principal disadvantages of the M-82F-powered 'Peshkas' were thought to be high fuel consumption, which significantly reduced range, and engine overheating through poor cooling. As a result of the latter trait it was necessary to pause periodically when climbing to allow the engines to cool down. Apart from that, the engines on each side of the aircraft reacted differently to a sharp injection of fuel, which prompted asymmetric acceleration that would cause the aircraft to swing during its takeoff run. This movement threatened to break the undercarriage.

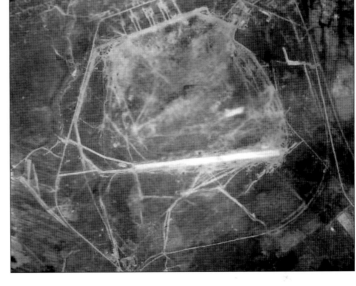

An aerial photo of a German airfield with a paved runway, taken by a high-flying Pe-2 crew in 1943

48th GvRAP was also issued with seven rare Pe-3s, manufactured by Factory No 22, in August-September 1944 to make good attrition.

It was during this period that the regiment was given the honorary title of 'Nizhnednestrovskiy'.

Amongst 48th GvRAP's most successful pilots in 1943-45 was 1 Lt Vladimir Chervyakov, who, by November 1943, had flown 102 photo-reconnaissance sorties surveying the enemy's most important assets. The following details were included in his service record;

'He was fired upon many times by anti-aircraft artillery and during attacks by enemy fighters, but thanks to an excellent flying technique and some skilful manoeuvres, he would return to his airfield and bring valuable information to the attention of command. He has carried out a series of special missions for Supreme High Command and has assimilated five aircraft types, amassing 410 flying hours.'

In a decree issued by the Presidium of the Supreme Soviet of the USSR dated 2 February 1944, pilot Vladimir Chervyakov was awarded the title of Hero of the Soviet Union. Having flown a further 59 long-range reconnaissance sorties in 1944, this courageous pilot completed his final wartime sortie on 9 May 1945.

98th GvRAP

In early autumn 1941, when the pre-war Soviet RAPs had lost virtually all of their aircraft, along with a considerable number of aircrew, a plan was conceived to attach a reconnaissance squadron to each of the fronts. These would be equipped with modern Pe-3 reconnaissance aircraft, the manufacture of these machines having commenced at Factory No 39 in Moscow in September 1941. Up until the middle of October, when the plant was forced to start relocating to Irkutsk, almost 200 Pe-3s had been completed. Some were sent to reconnaissance units, including the 215th RAE *(Razvedyvatel'naya Aviatsionnaya Eskadrilya* – Reconnaissance Air Squadron*)* led by

Capt S D Berman. It was decided that the squadron should be based at Monino, in the Moscow Region, where 2nd RAP of GK KA was already based.

Having begun combat operations on 25 October, initially with seven Pe-3s at its disposal, the unit had flown 90 combat sorties by the end of 1941, losing seven aircraft (four Pe-3s and three Pe-2s). Over the subsequent four months, from January to April 1942, a further 137 reconnaissance sorties were completed. In April the squadron was re-formed as 4th RAP, and Maj S D Berman was named as its commander. As of 1 May 1942 4th RAP of GK KA had 11 Pe-2s and eight Pe-3s at its disposal.

Now with three regiments under its command, Workers' and Peasants' Red Army Air Force headquarters ordered regular reconnaissance missions covering vast areas of the frontline and beyond, practically from 'sea to sea'.

To increase the depth of the territory surveyed by 4th RAP beyond the frontline, aside from its permanent base (Monino and, from November 1942, Chkalovskoye), the regiment began to apply the tactics used by operational groups, dispersing aircraft around operational airfields, namely Lipetsk, Yedrovo, Klin and others.

The unit's Pe-2s and Pe-3s were fitted with two AFA-1 aerial cameras each, but they were installed differently in each aircraft type. In the Pe-2 they were installed in the bomb-bay, while in the Pe-3 they were housed in the aft section of the fuselage. Later, from 1943-44, updated AFA-3S and AFA-33 aerial cameras replaced the AFA-1. Various pivoting installations with two camera positions were also used, which significantly increased the area that could be covered in a single approach.

In the summer of 1942 the reconnaissance crews of 4th RAP photographed an enemy formation of one Panzer and three armoured divisions in the Voronezh sector. In addition, an armoured column consisting of more than 500 units was discovered moving in the direction of Kharkov. Subsequently they succeeded in locating the central storage base for the German 6th Army. 4th RAP also surveyed the airfields at Smolensk, Bolbasovo, Vitebsk, Borovsk, Shatalovo, Seshcha and other locations on a weekly basis. Enemy road and rail movements in many different directions were also discovered and recorded. From the second half of 1942 onwards, filming the results of raids by long-range-bomber units became an additional mission. Typically, the range for a Pe-2 was 900 km (560 miles), while for the Pe-3 it was 1200 km (745 miles), and the maximum duration for the crew of the latter type exceeded four hours.

At the end of January 1943 Senior Battalion Commissar B P Artemyev became regimental commander. The 'Peshkas' were the principal combat aircraft in his regiment from mid-February 1943, 4th RAP having 22 Pe-2s and 6 Pe-3s on strength. It also had six camera-equipped Airacobras for tactical reconnaissance. By that time the regiment had flown 1204 combat sorties, its aircraft having been fired on by flak batteries and engaged by enemy fighters 52 times. Crews reported five German fighters destroyed, while losses to the regiment from interception by the Luftwaffe amounted to 27 aircraft destroyed and 19 pilots, navigators and air gunners killed.

Despite these heavy casualties, the regiment continued to fly critically important missions particularly in the lead up to the battle for the Kursk Salient. An operational group from 4th RAP consisting of two squadrons led by Maj Dmitriyev had departed for Kursk at the end of February 1943. Its zone of responsibility was to the west and southwest of Kursk (in the central sector). Crews duly carried out uninterrupted photography of this area on

Photographic technicians prepare an AFA-1 camera for installation in the bomb-bay of a Pe-2. The bomb-bay doors of photo-reconnaissance 'Peshkas' were bulged to reduce the effect of the slipstream on the camera lens

The crew of a Pe-2 reconnaissance aeroplane of 98th GvRAP. Note the lens of the AFA-33 aerial camera protruding from the bomb-bay, the external fuel tanks and the circular aerial of the RPK-10 'Chaenok' radio direction finder. During the second half of the war aircrews from the regiment operated in support of 16th Air Army and the 1st Byelorussian Front

three separate occasions – at the beginning and end of March and at the beginning of May 1943. The entire network of airfields around Orel, as well as the system of defensive structures, artillery and mortar positions and concentrations of tanks, armoured cars and vehicles were successfully recorded.

In May 1943 the second Kursk-based squadron set about conversion onto the A-20B. Shortly after this the third squadron in the regiment also received new Airacobras. On 17 June, not long before the start of the most critical battle of 1943 on the Soviet-German Front, a decree issued by People's Commissar for Defence I V Stalin transformed the regiment into 98th GvRAP of GK KA. In recognition of their service in combat with the regiment, squadron navigator Capt K I Stepin and section commanders 2Lts N I Yurkin and D F Lisitsin were made Heroes of the Soviet Union at the same time.

The regiment's operational groups subsequently saw action predominantly in the south of the Soviet-German Front. Crews from 98th GvRAP ensured that frontal command, having crossed the Dnepr and liberated Kiev and the entire right flank of the Ukraine, were supplied with intelligence. During the Korsun-Shevchenko operation, which resulted in two German army corps being surrounded, reconnaissance crews flew 355 combat sorties and succeeded in revealing the enemy's defensive system, as well as the location of artillery batteries and tank units.

Pilots who flew reconnaissance missions over enemy airfields in Pe-3s armed with a 20 mm gun did not deny themselves the pleasure of suddenly attacking enemy aircraft. Guards 1Lt Nikolayenko used the weapon to destroy a Ju 88 bomber from an altitude of 100 metres (300 ft) and then 'visited' the airfield at Vinnitsa and machine-gunned the aprons covered with aircraft.

During 1944 98th GvRAP carried out uninterrupted reconnaissance of defensive lines on the western bank of the River Visla, with the aim of crossing it and taking the base around Sandomir. In November of that year the regiment's operational group was redeployed to Lvov airfield, from where it would operate for the remainder of the war. That month, Guards Maj F F Zvontsov became regimental commander. Curiously, April 1945 turned out to be the most intensive month in the regiment's history, when the most combat sorties were flown – 449. The regiment flew its final mission on 11 May 1945.

FRONTLINE AIR RECONNAISSANCE REGIMENTS

In contrast to the three 'strategic' reconnaissance regiments previously mentioned, the following three aviation units became part of the air armies on different fronts and flew more mundane, though no less complicated, combat sorties.

The first of these regiments initially saw action as SB-equipped 32nd SBAP flying from Bada airfield in the Zabykalsk region. The 35 crews in the regiment saw action in China against the Japanese invaders, and fought the same enemy again during the Khalkhin-Gol conflict of 1939. 28th SAD was staffed by the more experienced crews, and 28 of them received government awards for the courage they had shown in combat with the Japanese.

On 22 June 1941 the regimental commander, Maj Artanenok, was ordered to immediately redeploy 32nd SBAP to the European part of the USSR. The first squadron was transferred to 150th SBAP shortly after its arrival in the city of Balashov, and three squadrons were formed from the remaining four. It was then that the regiment, consisting of 32 SBs, transferred to Starodub airfield, and combat operations against the advancing German forces began on 17 July. These were predominantly carried out during the day, without fighter cover.

On 24 July Maj Vedernikov was named regimental commander, and he led 32nd SBAP as it retreated east along with the Air Forces of 21st Army. In an effort to halt the losses being suffered by the regiment it switched to night operations from the middle of August. Fewer crews were indeed shot down from then on, but the regiment's combat effectiveness suffered too. 32nd SBAP handed over its six surviving SBs to 37th SBAP in early September and then departed for Balashov to regroup. In a little over two months of continuous fighting the regiment had flown 347 combat sorties, 130 of them at night.

At the end of October 1941 32nd SBAP completed its conversion to the Pe-3 heavy fighter. It was during this period, however, that the factory producing the aircraft began to evacuate to Irkutsk following the seemingly unstoppable German advance eastward, and it was out of action until March of the following year.

32nd SBAP was redeployed to the Zabaykal region, and it did not see action again until July 1942 as part of 284th BAD. With 21 Pe-2s on strength, it was committed to the heavy fighting on the Bryansk Front around Kastornaya-Voronezh-Zemlyansk. The regiment flew 177 bombing raids in 22 days, losing seven aircraft and eight aircrew. In accordance with an order from 15th Air Army command, from the beginning of August 1942 32nd SBAP switched completely to reconnaissance operations, which were flown by individual crews around Orel, Kursk and Stariy Oskol.

In early November 1942 crews from 32nd SBAP discovered that several dozen German twin-engined bombers landed at Kursk-vostochniy airfield at midday every day. This airfield was protected by flak batteries and fighters patrolling at various altitudes. On 9 November eight Il-2s suppressed the anti-aircraft fire while a second group of ground attack aircraft targeted the airfield from another direction. Enemy fighters appeared only during the ground attack aircrafts' final approach, and they were engaged by pilots of 225th ShAD (*Shturmovaya Aviatsionnaya Diviziya* – Ground Attack Air Division). The division's commander reported '40 enemy aircraft destroyed or damaged' to army headquarters, and this was confirmed by photographs taken by 32nd SBAP.

In an order from the commander of 15th Air Army, dated 24 November 1942, 32nd SBAP became a reconnaissance unit, and 15th ORAE (*Otdelnaya Razvedyvatel'naya Aviatsionnaya Eskadrilya* – Independent Reconnaissance Air Squadron), led by Maj N P Shchennikov, became part of this regiment. Shchernikov was immediately appointed commander of

32nd ORAP (*Otdel'niy Razvedyvatel'niy Aviatsionniy Polk* – Independent Reconnaissance Air Regiment).

During January and February 1943 the regiment repeatedly photographed the enemy's defensive positions in the sector between Bolkhov and Kastornaya. It was then engaged in active reconnaissance forward of the Bryansk Front until May. On the 4th of that month the regiment was given the honorary title 'Zabaykalsk', and on 17 June it became 99th GvORAP.

By August the regimental commander, Maj P I Gavrilov, had flown 130 reconnaissance missions, supplying command with valuable information on the enemy. In a decree from the Presidium of the Supreme Soviet of the USSR, dated 2 September 1943, Petr Gavrilov was made a Hero of the Soviet Union for his 'exemplary execution of combat missions, for command at the forefront of the battle against the German invaders and for the courage and heroism he has shown'.

Another outstanding character in 99th GvORAP at this time was Guards MSgt Nadezhda Aleksandrovna Zhurkina, a female radio-operator/gunner in a Pe-2 who flew 87 combat sorties during the course of the war. Having shot down one enemy aircraft and seriously damaged another, Zhurkina was one of the few women to be awarded all three classes of the Order of Glory, making her a Cavalier – in terms of status, a Cavalier of the full order is comparable with a Hero of the Soviet Union.

The successful offensive by Red Army forces on the Bryansk Front was completed in October 1943, and that month 15th Air Army (and 99th GvORAP) was transferred to the 2nd Baltic Front. At the end of February 1944 the regiment's crews began observing Idritsa airfield, establishing the number of enemy aircraft operating from the base, the location of its flak batteries and the general layout of its aprons. It became clear from their reports that there were no fewer than 90 aircraft based there, predominantly Ju 87s. The airfield was defended by dozens of flak batteries, operating in conjunction with anti-aircraft artillery at the nearby railway station and in the town of Idritsa itself.

The commander of 15th Air Army, Gen N F Naumenko, ordered a bombing raid to be carried out against the airfield, for which the photographic maps prepared by specialists in 99th GvORAP proved useful. The Chief of Staff of the Air Army, A A Sakovnin, subsequently reported;

'The raid on Irditsa airfield was carried out by two echelons between 1340-1400 hrs on 27 February 1944. The first echelon approached the airfield at low level from the southwest and began to attack from an altitude of 70 metres [230 ft]. The sun and the forest were used as camouflage and for the element of surprise, and the aircraft broke away from the target behind a wooded hill. The second echelon approached from the north at an

The commander (right) of a Pe-2 reconnaissance aircraft briefs his crew in preparation for a combat sortie. This machine has already seen some action – note the repair patch on the fuselage over the star insignia

altitude of 1200 metres [4,000 ft]. Following a sharp turn to the left, along with a reduction in altitude and a manoeuvre to evade anti-aircraft artillery, the attack began from an altitude of 400 metres [1300 ft]. The individual crews suppressed anti-aircraft artillery in the direction of the approaching ground attack aircraft.'

As a result of this strike on Irditsa airfield 32 enemy aircraft were destroyed or damaged. Battle damage reconnaissance at 1430 hrs reported up to 50 pockets of fire

either on the airfield or in the surrounding areas. Significantly, before 1300 hrs up to 80 passes by enemy aircraft on Soviet positions had been noted. After that time not one enemy bomber or reconnaissance aircraft appeared, even though the weather had improved.

Reconnaissance crews from 99th GvORAP, whose activities were gaining momentum as advancing Soviet troops neared German defensive positions on the 2nd Baltic Front, observed targets around the sites of future battles. The images captured by section commander 2Lt Viktor Bogutskiy's crew proved to be of particular value. Regimental commander Guards Lt Col N P Shchennikov noted;

'The enemy's systems and might over an area of 1117 km² (431 square miles) were revealed by Bogutskiy's crew during preparations by forces on the 2nd Baltic Front for their summer offensive.'

The reconnaissance crews were sometimes called upon to 'recall their past as bomber crews'. Thus, acting on an order from the commander of 15th Air Army dated 8 August 1944, a group of nine Pe-2s from 99th GvORAP carried out a dive-bombing attack on a bridge at Krustpils, which they destroyed.

In the concluding phase of the war 99th GvORAP participated in the rout of the Wehrmacht's Kurland formation, and carried out reconnaissance of the convoys travelling between Germany and the Baltic. The regiment was transferred to the Leningrad Front at the beginning of March 1945, where it remained through to war's end. 99th GvORAP had completed more than 3000 combat sorties during the conflict, of which 2475 were reconnaissance missions, and it lost around 100 aircraft and 188 aircrew.

Officers of 99th GvORAP who received awards come together for a group photograph. Behind them is a rare version of the Pe-2 powered by M-82F air-cooled radial engines. Small batches of this variant were built in late 1943 and early 1944, and almost all of them were delivered to reconnaissance units

164th GvORAP

On 25 July 1941 a regiment comprising two squadrons from 25th BAD's 18th Red Banner SBAP was formed on Kutaisi airfield in Georgia. 18-A SBAP was led by Maj N M Stetsenko and the regiment was equipped with 19 SBs and a single USB training aircraft. The policy of dividing large-scale pre-war regiments such as 18th SBAP (which was comprised of 60+ aircraft) was implemented after early-war experience had shown that such units were too large to base on a single operational airfield. Overcrowding at bases by these large regiments had resulted in them incurring significant losses during early air raids by enemy aircraft.

Armament technicians install a UBK 12.7 mm large-calibre machine gun in the nose compartment of a Pe-2 reconnaissance aeroplane

18-A SBAP was quickly renamed 366th SBAP in August 1941, and it subsequently participated in the Iranian operation that saw British and Soviet forces occupy the country because of the threat posed by pro-German factions in the region. The regiment remained in the Caucasus until early October 1941, when General Paul von Kleist's Panzer group threatened to take Rostov-On-Don. From 10 October to 29 December 366th SBAP, led by Capt A S Mozgovoy, flew 381 combat sorties, destroying 344 vehicles, up to 65 tanks and 15 artillery emplacements. According to crew reports, 14 enemy fighters were destroyed in aerial combat. The unit's losses amounted to 12 SBs and 30 aircrew.

In early 1942 366th SBAP saw action on the Southern Front. This was one of the most intense sectors in the battle against the Germans during this period. Withdrawing to the North Caucasus along with the ground troops, the regiment (which converted to the Pe-2 at this time) subsequently inflicted heavy losses on the enemy, completing 1059 combat sorties in 'Peshkas' up to 12 February 1942. Crews destroyed more than 1300 vehicles, 171 tanks and two trains, and shot down eight aircraft. In the six months from January to June 1942 the regiment lost 20 Pe-2s and 32 aircrew.

On 4 October 1942 two 'Peshkas' from 366th SBAP, led by Maj I K Boronin, made a long-range flight from their airfield near Grozniy, along the Great Caucasian Ridge to Pyatigorsk. Here, they bombed the local theatre and the Hotel Bristol, where, according to information from partisans, an award ceremony for Hitler's officers was underway. The raid took place in twilight, but the target was rocked by a series of explosions. The return flight was made in total darkness, both aircraft landing safely after flying over mountainous terrain.

By this time Maj Boronin had flown 156 combat sorties, of which 45 were reconnaissance missions and 111 bombing and ground attack raids on concentrations of enemy forces. In a decree issued by the Presidium of the Supreme Soviet of the USSR, dated 13 December 1942, Ivan Boronin was awarded the title of Hero of the Soviet Union for 'his exemplary execution of combat missions, for command and for the courage and heroism he has shown at the forefront of the battle with the German invaders'. The new commander of 366th SBAP, Maj A P Bardeyev, was similarly honoured in the same decree. Incidentally, it was at this time that the term 'bomber' in relation to the regiment's title became a thing of the past, the unit becoming 366th ORAP via a decree from Air Force headquarters.

The regiment recorded some noteworthy achievements whilst performing reconnaissance missions. For example, in November 1942 crews established that two German Panzer divisions (23rd Panzer and the SS Viking Division) had been withdrawn from Mozdok and transferred to Kotelnikovo.

Amongst the personnel who distinguished themselves in 1942-43 was 9th ORAE pilot 2Lt S V Yatskovskiy, who was subsequently made a Hero of the Soviet Union. His recommendation for this award read as follows;

'On 27 April 1943 comrade Yatskovskiy, while carrying out reconnaissance of enemy forces on the Taman and Crimean peninsulas, discovered and photographed up to 200 aircraft of different types on Bagerovo airfield, up to 50 Me 109F aircraft on Anapa airfield and up to 30 Ju 87 aircraft on Gostagayevsky airfield. He then photographed the port of Taman, in which 15 high-speed landing barges and eight motorised pontoons were moored.

'During the spring and summer of 1943 comrade Yatskovskiy demonstrated exemplary aerial reconnaissance. He revealed and photographed the entire multi-layered "Blue Line" defence and the enemy's defences along the eastern coast of the Kerch peninsula during a mission ordered by 4th Air Army command.'

366th ORAP flew 1218 combat sorties in 1943. Regimental losses amounted to eight Pe-2s and seven A-20Bs, and 13 pilots, 14 navigators and 21 gunners were killed.

The regiment continued to fight in the southern sector of the Soviet-German Front until May 1944, participating in the liberation of the Crimea. On 14 April that year 366th SBAP became 164th GvORAP, and ten days later it was given the honorary title 'Kerchensk'.

Crews widely used oblique aerial photography in the final year of the war, which significantly reduced the loss rate that had previously afflicted the regiment. Oblique photography removed the need for aircraft to have to fly directly over the target, where they were exposed to its defensive anti-aircraft artillery. The regiment lost just five Pe-2s and eight aircrew in the whole of 1944.

On 5 April 1945 the GvORAP was awarded the Order of the Red Banner for exemplary command reconnaissance, and for the part it played in the liberation of the city of Elblag.

193rd GvORAP

In April 1938 the 50th SBAP was formed around a cadre of personnel from 4th High-Speed Bomber Squadron at Siverskaya airfield, near Leningrad. By the time combat operations commenced against Finland in the Winter War in late 1939, the regiment had 60 SBs and 46 combat-ready crews at its disposal. From 6 January it operated from the ice airfield

A Pe-2 of 164th GvORAP prepares for takeoff. This regiment was originally formed in the Caucasus as 366th SBAP, which then became 366th RAP, and it received its Guards honorary name in May 1944. From December 1942 until war's end the regiment was commanded by Lt Col Aleksander Bardeev. Smiling crew commander Yatskovskiy, at the controls of this Pe-2, displays a clean-shaven face in defiance of the superstition that discouraged pilots from shaving before a combat sortie

An aerial photograph of a German airfield in Pomerania, taken by a Pe-2 crew from 164th GvORAP. In addition to the three He 111s that are clearly visible, a jet aircraft can also be seen on the runway threshold. Although Soviet photo interpreters identified it as a Me 163, it is in fact a Heinkel He 162 *Volksjäger*

on the Sestroretsk overflow, flying 2321 sorties and losing 13 aircrew during the course of its combat operations. 50th SBAP was awarded the Order of the Red Banner for courage in the line of duty, and ten airmen (four posthumously), including the regimental commander and military commissar, were awarded the title of Hero of the Soviet Union.

50th SBAP was redeployed to Ungra airfield, in Estonia, in August 1940, where it came under the control of 4th SAD of the Air Forces of the Baltic military district. As of 22 June 1941 there were 33 SBs (including six unserviceable machines) and five Pe-2s in service with the regiment, although crews had yet to be properly trained on the latter type. On that day 50th SBAP, led by Lt Col F A Agaltsov, flew two sorties – one at midday using three groups of nine SBs to attack enemy columns around Taurage, and another which began at twilight, when aircraft began taking off for a night raid on the cities of Konigsberg, Tilzit and Istenburg. Only 11 aircraft reached the target, the others being subjected to a sudden attack by enemy fighters. They downed 21 SBs in just 30 minutes.

Having lost most of its aircraft, the regiment was sent to the rear on 1 July 1941, where it was issued with 30 Pe-2s. Soon back in action, 50th SBAP lost 17 of 20 Pe-2s sent to bomb a vehicle column to the north of Yelnya on 9 August as a result of attacks by enemy fighters and fire from small-calibre artillery and machine guns. Following this one-sided action, it became clear to VVS RKKA that the Pe-2 was not a ground-attack aircraft, as it was quite vulnerable to flak at low level. However, on this occasion it was Bf 109s that inflicted most losses. Subsequently, aircraft from 50th SBAP flew to their targets escorted by MiG-3 fighters. This frontline tour also turned out to be a short one, as the regiment was sent to regroup once again on 11 September 1941.

50th SBAP remained away from the action until 12 June 1942, when the regiment (which had now become part of 223rd SAD of 2nd Air Army) set off on a bombing raid against the enemy on the Voronezh Front. The German summer offensive in the southern sector of the Soviet-German Front was by then well underway, its mechanised troops being supported by significant Luftwaffe forces. As in the previous year, the Bf 109s quickly achieved air superiority, and this meant that the Soviet bomber units would again suffer heavy losses.

On 4 and 5 July five 'Peshkas' from 50th SBAP were shot down by German fighters close to Dmitriyevskiy-Chertkov. However, 2nd Air Army Headquarters still continued to send the dive-bombers on missions as the enemy's tanks had to be destroyed, as did their river-spanning crossing points. Three times, on 25, 28 and 29 July, 50th SBAP used precision bombing raids to destroy bridges and crossing points used by the enemy. A week later, on 6 August, a formation of five 'Peshkas' led by squadron commander Capt S I Zlatoverkhovnikov struck a concentration of trains at Zapadnaya Kastornaya in a dive-bombing attack.

Despite the heavy losses of this period, there was no shortage of experienced and competent crews in 50th SBAP. Indeed, the regiment managed to fly 510 combat sorties between 12 July and the end of November.

On 12 December the unit became a detached reconnaissance regiment, and it was at this point that 324th ORAE, led by Capt Zhdanov, joined the ranks.

In early February 1943 A Skopin's crew was tasked with photographing the airfield and freight yard at Poltava. According to information provided by agents, the Germans were training new bomber crews on the base, while military equipment was being transported on trains loaded at the local freight yard. The enemy was taken completely by surprise when the 'Peshka' arrived over Poltava airfield, the photographs taken by the crew revealing more than 100 bombers on the ground and up to 12 aircraft engaged in training flights, performing continuous circuits. The Pe-2 returned to base

An external fuel tank is attached to the centre section of a photo-reconnaissance Pe-2. The tank could only be used for two flights at most because its cardboard construction meant that it could not sustain contact with fuel for too long

as quickly as possible, and the following night groups of long-range bombers carried out effective raids on both the airfield and the freight yard.

On 12 August 1943 Lt M L Solovyov, commanding a wing of 50th ORAP, discovered a column of 20 tanks moving towards Trostyanets. The following day movement of enemy tanks and armoured vehicles was again noted in the same general location, and reconnaissance aircraft duly photographed a column of 50 tanks heading towards Akhtyrka. This information, together with other intelligence collected by Solovyov, allowed Command to suggest that the enemy was preparing a counterattack, and commanders on the Voronezh Front sent fresh forces to aid the threatened units. The enemy was driven back by heavy bombing raids and was then routed.

On 4 January 1944 Mikhail Solovyov was ordered to carry out reconnaissance of enemy airfields around Belaya Tserkov and Umani. Taking off in the morning, he crossed the frontline at high altitude. Descending to 1000 metres (3300 ft), he photographed Umansk airfield, which was home to 55 enemy aircraft. Solovyov's Pe-2 was then attacked by three Bf 109s close to Belaya Tserkov, but countering their persistent attacks by manoeuvring and using cloud cover, Solovyov managed to escape and land his damaged aircraft safely, delivering some very valuable information to frontline command.

In the course of a year of combat operations Solovyov captured on camera 1000 tanks, 28,000 vehicles, 1600 aircraft on airfields, 760 trains at stations, two armoured regiments and 15,000 wagons. On 26 October 1944 he was made a Hero of the Soviet Union for carrying out 122 reconnaissance sorties against the enemy, and for demonstrating courage and heroism. Solovyov failed to return from a sortie on 23 November 1944.

In the spring of 1944, while Soviet forces were advancing along the eastern edge of the Ukraine, reconnaissance flights had to be made under difficult conditions. Fog, rain and wet snow were commonplace, and mists hung just above the ground. Despite this, on 5 April, crews from 50th ORAP found a column of 50 tanks and 500 vehicles moving from Stanislav to Chortkov and another column of 800 vehicles moving from Galich to Pidhaitsi. On 22 April (the day that Lt Col G G Bystrov was made commander of 50th ORAP), the regiment had two squadrons equipped with Pe-2s in its line-up, as well as one flying Il-2 ground attack aircraft.

In the second half of the summer, while participating in the Lvov-Sandomir offensive operation by the 1st Ukrainian Front, the regiment flew 960 combat sorties. The outcome of this operation was the complete routing of Army Group Northern Ukraine, which ceased to exist. The contribution of 50th ORAP to this success was recognised at the highest levels. On 19 August 1944 the regiment became 193rd GvORAP and was awarded the honorary title 'Lvov'. During 1944 the regiment flew more than 2000 combat sorties and lost 13 Pe-2s and six Il-2s.

Subsequently, 193rd GvORAP fought as part of 2nd Air Army right up to the end of the war in Europe, participating in the Vislensk and Berlin offensive operations and in the liberation of Prague. Crews from 193rd GvORAP flew 861 combat sorties during 1945, and suffered grievous losses during the final four months of the war – ten Pe-2s and seven Il-2s. It was only after the fighting was over that the regiment received another award, the Order of Kutuzov, 3rd degree, on 4 June 1945.

GUARDS BOMBER AIR REGIMENTS OF NAVAL AIR FORCES

Two Naval Air Forces regiments equipped with the Pe-2 were awarded the title of Guards Regiments during the war. The first was 73rd BAP of the Baltic Fleet Air Force, formed in August 1940 by Hero of the Soviet Union Col A I Krokalev. He was subsequently relieved of his command on 14 November 1940 owing to a high accident rate. Maj F M Koptev replaced him, but Krokalev returned as CO on 9 August 1941 after his replacement was hospitalised with serious injuries after yet another flying accident.

Prior to the German invasion of June 1941, 73rd BAP was equipped with some 60 aircraft (Ar-2s and SBs) as part of 10th BAB, based at Pyarnu and Koporie airfields. On 8 July 73rd BAP flew to Kerstovo, only to return to its home airfields ten days later with orders to protect the Baltic Fleet's main base near Tallinn.

Although most of the 'Peshkas' initially sent to the Baltic region were issued to 57th BAP, 73rd BAP had received four Pe-2s by early July. These were mainly used for the reconnaissance of ground targets in the vicinity of Tallinn.

On 19-23 August the regiment was redeployed to an airfield near Leningrad. Here, it became part of 8th Air Brigade, and was tasked with striking advancing German troops who had broken through the Luga defensive line. The number of aircraft available to 73rd BAP decreased rapidly, and by the beginning of September there were only 12-15 SBs and Ar-2s left serviceable. One of the aircraft lost to Bf 109s in late August was the Ar-2 flown by Col Anatoliy Krokalev. However, he and his navigator 2Lt Dmitriy Fomin managed to bail out.

In accordance with a decision by Command dated 24 September 1941, 73rd BAP was withdrawn from the front to be strengthened and convert to the Pe-2 dive-bomber. This period passed without any accidents or serious incidents in flight, despite numerous mock dive-bombing runs being made. With a total of 20 crews having been cleared to fly the aircraft in combat, the regiment was sent to Irkutsk in May 1942 to collect its new aircraft. A month later 73rd BAP returned to a base near Leningrad.

From July 1942 crews from the regiment took part in the battle to capture the island of Sommers, in the Gulf of Finland. The German depot ship *Nettelbeck* and the Finnish gunboat *Turunmaa* were damaged by shrapnel as a result of continuous raids by the 'Peshkas'. Pilots Maj D Ya

On 21 May 1943 a Pe-2 crew of 73rd BAP of the Baltic Fleet Air Force failed to return from a combat mission after attacking the railway bridge at Narva. Its crew comprised pilot Aleksander Chubenidze (left), navigator Leonid Moshkar (centre) and radio-operator/gunner Kuzma Posudnevskiy (right). The pilot and navigator died in the crash and the wounded radio-operator/gunner was killed on the ground by German soldiers

Nemchneko and Maj F E Sayenko and navigators Capts N I Grigoryev and D N Fomin distinguished themselves during these raids.

On 20 August regimental CO Col Krokalev departed for a new posting, and 73rd BAP came under the command of Lt Col M A Kurochkin. He oversaw a subsequent augmentation of equipment and personnel that turned 73rd BAP into a mixed regiment for a few months, with two squadrons of low-powered U-2 biplanes operating alongside two squadrons of Pe-2s and two squadrons of obsolete Neman R-10 light bombers. It was with this motley collection of equipment that the regiment took part in Operation *Iskra* to break the siege of Leningrad.

During the preparatory period for this campaign the regiment struck enemy forces and strongpoints along a wide front, diverting attention from the areas where the breakthrough would take place. After the ground forces had begun to advance, the air component concentrated its efforts on striking fortifications on the Sinyavino Heights.

German artillery housed in the 8th Hydroelectric Station was a particular hindrance to advancing Red Army units. Covered on both sides by high passes, the power station looked like an ancient fortress from the outside. It soon became clear that only heavy aerial bombardment could destroy the power station's main building. The bombs would have to be dropped in such a way that the infantry entrenched nearby would not be harmed. The shadow of the power station that was projected onto the walls on either side of the site clearly revealed the location of the artillery. Moreover, crews of 73rd BAP had crossed the frontline in this region many times, and had studied the locality well. The guns were knocked out during the course of a single mission against the power station.

The regiment had to tackle an even more complex challenge in May 1943 – to destroy the railway bridge across the River Narva. In accordance with instructions given by Kurochkin, the regiment's elite 'sniper squadron' trained on a specially equipped range for one week prior to targeting the bridge. Each crew carried out no fewer than three practice bombing runs on a 15-metre by 100-metre (50 ft x 330 ft) target, which replicated the dimensions of the actual bridge.

From 12 to 14 May the squadron, led by 2Lt V S Golubev, dive-bombed the target on three occasions, pulling out to level flight at an altitude of about 700-800 metres (2300-2625 ft). Fighter attacks were successfully repelled, but the bad weather and heavy artillery fire over the target

Aircrew of the second squadron, 73rd BAP, come together for a group photograph during the winter of 1943-44

(there were four small-calibre and two medium-calibre anti-aircraft batteries defending the site) prevented completion of the mission – there were no direct hits.

A fourth raid took place on the morning of 21 May, when three aircraft dropped four FAB-250 bombs each, while the others expended two or three FAB-100s and

The longed-for target of the Baltic Fleet Air Force was the Finnish coastal defence destroyer *Vainamoinen*, which was the country's largest warship. The ship barely participated in combat, however, and it did not play any specific role in Baltic sea battles during World War 2. Nevertheless, the Soviet command hoped to demoralise the enemy by sinking it

FAB-250s – 700-800 kg (1540-1760 lb) for each 'Peshka'. This time the bombs were on target and the bridge was destroyed. Movements along the Tallinn-Gachina route were interrupted for 28 hours. However, uncoordinated attacks by enemy fighters brought down two 'Peshkas', killing the crews of P A Vedeneyev and A I Chubinidze, and others were seriously damaged.

73rd BAP achieved its greatest notoriety in the Baltic region when Maj Vasiliy Ivanovich Rakov became a squadron commander. A graduate of the Kachinsk and Sevastopol flying schools, he distinguished himself as commander of the 57th SBAP during the Winter War with Finland, after which he became a Hero of the Soviet Union. He then entered the academy to study, and following graduation at the beginning of 1942 was sent to the Air Forces of the Black Sea Fleet. He was persistent in refining his tactical and flying training, and commanded both units and individual formations. During the concluding phase of the defence of Sevastopol, Col Rakov was a deputy commander of 3rd Special Air Group. He then commanded 13th SBAP, but was removed from this post and demoted to major following two accidents. Rakov was eventually sent to 73rd BAP as a squadron commander.

In January 1944 73rd BAP became 12th GvBAP. From that month onwards, and with Rakov's direct participation, the regiment set about mastering dive-bombing raids as a flight. The celebrated pilot recalled;

'The formation stretches slightly when recovering from a dive and it is difficult to maintain position. One can feel the g-loads – if one tries to raise an arm or a leg it is as though a weight weighing two pounds has been tied to it. If a man weighs say 70-80 kg [150-175 lbs], then as he pulls out of a dive his weight literally increases to 400 kg [880 lbs]. One is pushed back in the seat and there are stars in your eyes. However, it is far better to be sitting in the pilot's seat than that of the navigator or gunner. The g-load is easier to bear if one is sitting down. The navigator and gunner, though, are mostly standing up, and have to move the machine gun in the standing position.

The distinctive outline of the hull and the single funnel of the German anti-aircraft depot ship *Niobe*, the former Dutch coastal defence destroyer *Gelderland*, contributed to the vessel's misidentification as *Vainamoinen*. However, the positioning and calibre of the warship's weaponry was completely different from that of the Finnish vessel

'In the first years of the war aircraft would dive onto the target on their own, and enemy fighters would join them by flying below and slightly behind them, anticipating the right moment to shoot the bomber down. Dive-bombing as a flight was more dangerous for intercepting fighters.'

The legendary Maj Vasiliy Rakov, commander of 12th GvBAP, in the cockpit of a Pe-2. Note the lines painted on the canopy sides, which the pilot used to maintain the desired diving angle by aligning them with the horizon

It was not easy for the dive-bomber crews to fend off attacks by heavily armed Fw 190s, not least because the enemy fighters had a significant advantage in terms of speed (100 km/h (60 mph) or more). Moreover, the Pe-2 could not fly far on one engine. Thus, alongside the successful bombing raids, carried out with no losses, there were the unsuccessful ones in which significant numbers of Pe-2s were shot down. For example, four Pe-2s from 12th GvBAP failed to return from an attack on a German convoy at sea on 17 May 1944. One of those aircraft was flown by 2Lt Yuriy Kosenko, who crashed into the water not far from the Finnish naval base at Khamin. Flying his 76th sortie, Kosenko was posthumously awarded the title of Hero of the Soviet Union.

During early July 1944 Soviet intelligence detected a large warship in the Finnish port of Kotka. It was identified as the coastal defence ship *Vainamoinen*, the Finnish Navy's largest warship, but it was in fact the German heavy anti-aircraft depot ship *Niobe*. Originally built for the Dutch Navy as the coastal defence destroyer *Gelderland*, *Niobe* had a similar appearance and displacement to *Vainamoinen*. In accordance with instructions from the People's Commissariat of the Navy Adm N G Kuznetsov, preparations began for a simultaneous mass attack on the vessel led by Gen M I Samokhin of the Red Banner Air Forces of the Baltic Fleet.

This was to be an assault by four air groups, consisting of 133 aircraft, and they were to carry out their bombing runs within a narrow seven-minute window. The aircraft were divided into specific groups, with some suppressing flak batteries and others acting as decoys. There would also be a powerful fighter presence. The principal task of sinking the ship was assigned to 24 Pe-2s led by 12th GvBAP CO Maj V I Rakov and four A-20Gs led by Maj I N Ponomarenko.

The vessel was attacked with clinical precision on 16 July, *Niobe* being hit by as many as ten large bombs that left the ship burning. According to reports from returning bomber crews, the vessel broke up and sank. Soon after he had returned from the mission, Maj Rakov was promoted to the rank of colonel. By war's end he had flown 172 combat sorties, of which around 100 were in the Pe-2, and participated in the sinking of 12 ships. Rakov was the first aviator in both 12th GvBAP and the Red Banner Air Forces of the Baltic Fleet to have been twice awarded the title of Hero of the Soviet Union.

Following the encirclement of the huge German formation in Kurland, the trading port and base at Liepaja took on particular significance for the besieged Wehrmacht. Troops were brought in through this location, and up to 30 transports would be loaded simultaneously. Making use of some

A Pe-2 of the second squadron, 12th GvBAP, in winter camouflage. This is a late-series bomber with the antennae mast relocated to the windscreen frame and individual engine exhaust stubs. Note that this aircraft has its tactical number painted on the fuselage, which was a feature unique to naval regiments. VVS RKKA Pe-2 units usually applied this number to the vertical tails of their aircraft

favourable flying weather, aircraft of the Naval Air Forces set about bombing Liepaja. To protect it, the Germans had concentrated 17 medium-calibre and 12 small-calibre flak batteries (up to 200 guns) at the site. The vessels moored in the bay off Liepaja also used their own anti-aircraft weaponry to fire on Soviet bombers. However, the real threat was from enemy fighters based on nearby airfields.

Soviet aircraft suffered heavy losses in the early attacks on Liepaja, ten Pe-2s and three Yak-9s being shot down in an aerial battle over the harbour on 10 October – five of the 'Peshka' crews were killed. One of those who failed to return was Capt Yuriy A Kozhevnikov, a squadron commander from 12th GvBAP. It later emerged that his bomber had been seriously damaged in an air battle with Fw 190s, but the pilot was still able to drop his bombs accurately. The aircraft was then hit by an artillery round and caught fire. It was too low for the crew to bail out, so Kozhevnikov landed in a clearing behind enemy lines. Radio-operator/gunner Snr Sgt N A Sazonov helped the injured pilot and the navigator, 2Lt V I Melnikov, out of the cockpit. Unfortunately Kozhevnikov was killed in the crossfire while crossing the frontline, but the navigator and gunner returned to their unit following treatment and a period of recovery.

In an effort to reduce losses over Liepaja, the Soviet Command hastily conducted training in tactical flying – this included formation bombing practice on a range and techniques for fending off attacks by Fw 190s. Following the completion of this training, the Soviets planned to attack targets in Liepaja simultaneously using naval dive-bombers, ground attack aircraft and torpedo-bombers. The operation, codenamed *Arcturus*, incorporated several mass attacks scheduled for different dates. Each raid would vary from the previous one in terms of the aircraft used and the tactics they employed.

On 30 October, for example, the ground attack aircraft were the first to arrive over the target, escorted by fighters. Although the Il-2s managed to attract the attention of a group of Fw 190s, the German pilots could not be drawn away from intercepting the main attack group. As 30 Pe-2s and eight A-20G torpedo-bombers, escorted by 43 Yak-9s, drew nearer, some of the Fw 190s turned on them. Nine 'Peshkas' and two Bostons failed to return to their airfields, and one damaged Pe-2 was sent for repair following an

For much of the war naval pilot Capt Aleksander Gnedoy served with 40th SBAP of the Black Sea Fleet Air Force, with whom he was awarded the title of Hero of the Soviet Union. When operations in the Black Sea ended, he was transferred to the Baltic region to join 12th GvBAP

emergency landing. According to reports from Soviet crews, three transport vessels with a combined displacement of around 16,000 tonnes (15,750 tons) were sunk during the raid.

German sources state that fighters of I. and II./JG 54 achieved extraordinary successes in air battles over Liepaja during this period, some 50-55 Fw 190s typically being sent aloft to counter each of the raids. The Luftwaffe indicated that the most successful pilot on 27 October was the commander of 2./JG 54, Oberleutnant Otto Kittel. He allegedly secured seven victories in three sorties, reporting that he had shot down two Yak-9s, three Il-2s and two Pe-2s. Less than half of these victories are confirmed in Soviet records, however. Three days later German fighter pilots really did operate quite effectively, claiming 15 Pe-2s destroyed – II./JG 54 was credited with 12 of them. As previously noted, in reality nine 'Peshkas' were destroyed on this date.

Capt A F Kalinichenko led a group of 22 Pe-2s during the final raid of Operation *Arcturus*, carried out in fine weather on 22 December. 12th GvBAP pilot Andrey Filippovich recalled;

'We were met over Liepaja by bursts of anti-aircraft artillery. The city was shrouded in smoke and dust. Our ground attack aircraft that went in two minutes ahead of us had thinned the ranks of Hitler's air defence forces substantially. They didn't even allow some of the flak batteries to fire a single shot.

'The day before it had been decided that the principal strike should be on the commercial port, where the greatest number of enemy transports had gathered. Remembering the order from divisional commander M A Kurochkin, I tried as much as possible to lead a tightly packed group against the target. The anti-aircraft artillery intensified as the aircraft turned onto a combat heading. I thought to myself, "Evidently the ground attack aircraft did their job and departed".

'There followed 30 to 40 seconds of extreme stress for the crew. I had to maintain the flight pattern as much as possible while the navigator took aim. The "Peshka" passed over the target itself. It was at that moment that the anti-aircraft artillery started to fire more accurately. The rounds were exploding right next to us, and I felt an urge to pull the aircraft off to the side somewhere, but somehow I held my nerve and suppressed my instinct of self-defence. The group of nine dived as one, each onto its own target. Some of the bombs fell on the quay, while the rest of them covered a large transport. One minute later a group of eight torpedo-bombers appeared over the target, having emerged from the direction of the open sea. They rushed past in a low-level whirlwind and suddenly attacked the transports moored in the outer harbour. Three huge explosions leapt into the air.

Pe-2s of 12th GvBAP taxi out over compacted snow in preparation for takeoff. The radio-operator/gunners in both aircraft are standing on the fuselage floors of their Pe-2s, monitoring the bombers' progress and ready to warn their pilots in the event of any danger (marauding Luftwaffe fighters, for example) during manoeuvres on the ground

'The dive-bombers had set a warehouse in the port ablaze and sunk a large transport vessel, the latter laden down with both troops and various items of equipment. However, successes such as these came at a high price, for we lost one of the most highly trained and battle hardened crews that day when the Pe-2 of 2Lt F N Menyailov failed to return.

'Documents record that one of the most dangerous enemies for our pilots was the Fw 190, which downed four Pe-2s and two Yak-9s over Liepaja that day. A further three "Peshkas" fell victim to anti-aircraft fire.'

This Pe-2, flown by the CO of 12th GvBAP, Maj Vasiliy Rakov, had specific markings in the form of the Guards emblem on the nose and three-dimensional star insignia, but no tactical number. Note the airborne Po-2 liaison biplane visible above the centre fuselage of the aircraft

Official Soviet Statistics for Operation *Arcturus*

Date of raid	Number of aircraft taking part	Number of ground attack aircraft	Number of Pe-2s	Total aircraft losses	Number of enemy vessels sunk
27 October	130	56	32	10	1 tanker
28 October	142	70	25	7	1 transport
30 October	148	68	30	15	2 transports
14 December	175	83	27	16	6 transports and 1 tanker
22 December	180	74	26	14	3 transports
Totals	775	351	140	62	12 transports and 2 tankers

In addition to the vessels listed above that were sunk, 13 transports, one minesweeper, two torpedo boats and one landing barge were certainly damaged.

According to the Germans, the results announced by Soviet pilots were exaggerated. It follows from German documents that ground attack aircraft inflicted the most damage. Thus, on 30 October, two transports were damaged by direct hits and caught fire (the fires were extinguished by the Germans), and a further transport was damaged by shrapnel. On the same day a hospital ship, three tugs, a minesweeper and a coast guard vessel were damaged, and a fire ship was sunk by torpedo-bombers. On 14 December two transports were damaged by direct hits from bombs and another was damaged by a nearby explosion. Six transports, a tug and a minesweeper were slightly damaged by shrapnel and machine gun fire.

Reports reveal that 18 Pe-2s from 12th GvBAP were destroyed around Liepaja during the course of *Arcturus* – five missions on five different dates. The unit's losses in the fourth year of the war (48 'Peshkas', predominantly to enemy fighters) were greater than in the first year of the war. The regiment lost 29 Pe-2s in the last three months of 1944 alone. Nevertheless, its combat

Aircrew from 34th BAP of the Pacific Fleet Air Force prepares for their next sortie from Nikolayevka. The regiment received the Guards designation in late August 1945 after it had helped defeat Japan

readiness remained at a high level. The regiment, which ended the war attacking vessels in Pillau harbour, was awarded the Order of the Red Banner and the Order of Ushakov and given the honorary title 'Tallinn'.

34th GvBAP

34th BAP of the Air Forces of the Pacific Fleet formed in 1938 in the Far East, the regiment being assigned 52nd and 53rd BAEs equipped with SBs. Based at Nikolayevka airfield, it was part of 29th AB (*Aviatsionnaya Brigada* – Air Brigade), and from March 1942 it came under 10th AB of the Air Forces of the Pacific Fleet. Seeing no action until the summer of 1945, by the start of combat operations against Japan in August of that year, the regiment was led by Capt (later Maj) N I Druzdev. On 9 August the regiment had 63 Pe-2s (of which 36 were airworthy) and one Tu-2 at its disposal. These aircraft were assigned to 36 crews, almost all of whom had no combat experience. Squadron CO Capt G V Pasynkov was the only exception, as he had been made a Hero of the Soviet Union in May 1944 whilst serving as a member of 12th GvBAP. He had been posted to the Air Forces of the Pacific Fleet as a result of staff rotation.

34th BAP prepared for battle carefully, and the raids on vessels in Rasin harbour on 9-10 August 1945 had a positive effect. The regiment flew 81 combat sorties and reported that five transport vessels had been sunk. During an airborne operation from 13-17 August to capture the port of Seisin, the regiment managed to negate Japanese resistance with several mass raids against their defensive positions. It is recorded that the dive-bombers flew 180 combat sorties in this period (more than half of which were flown by 34th BAP), dropping 85 tonnes (84 tons) of bombs of various calibres. Amongst the targets hit was the railway station in Seisin, which was destroyed, as was railway track up to a distance of 100 metres (330 ft) from the station. Nearby offices, a depot and two oil petroleum storage areas were also successfully bombed. Finally, a local workshop of the Mitsubishi company and 16 related buildings were also destroyed.

A solitary Pe-2 was shot down by anti-aircraft fire during operations to bomb the railway stations, the crew ditching successfully in Seisin harbour. On 9 August 1945 another bomber made an emergency landing behind its own lines owing to a lack of fuel while returning from a mission. The aircraft broke up and all three aircrew were injured. There were no recorded losses due to Japanese fighter activity.

The recommendation for the title of Guards regiment, signed by the Military Council of the Pacific Fleet and ratified on 26 August 1945, stated that 34th BAP had flown 221 combat sorties during the course of the war with Japan. It had inflicted much damage on the enemy in the ports of Yuki, Rasin and Seisin, where it had sunk two freighters and two tankers. In the cities of Ranan and Funej an armoured train, three warehouses and more than 30 railway wagons were destroyed and an anti-aircraft battery put out of action.

The regiment became the 34th GvBAP of the Air Forces of the Pacific Fleet.

APPENDICES

SCHEME OF Pe-2 GUARDS UNITS TRANSITION

1941	1942	1943	1944	1945

Bomber units of Red Army Air Force

1941	1942	1943	1944	1945
31st SBAP	4th Guards BAP			
5th SBAP	8th Guards BAP			
44th SBAP		34th Guards BAP		
	514th BAP	36th Guards BAP		
99th SBAP		96th Guards BAP		
137th SBAP		114th Guards BAP		

3rd Guards BAD

1941	1942	1943	1944	1945
2nd SBAP		119th Guards BAP		
130th SBAP		122nd Guards BAP		
261st SBAP		123rd Guards BAP		

1st Guards BAK
4th Guards BAD

1941	1942	1943	1944	1945
10th SBAP		124th Guards BAP		
	587th SBAP	125th Guards BAP		
224th SBAP		126th Guards BAP		

5th Guards BAD

1941	1942	1943	1944	1945
150th SBAP	35th Guards BAP			
134th SBAP		127th Guards BAP		
205th SBAP		128th Guards BAP		

6th Guards BAD

1941	1942	1943	1944	1945
33rd SBAP	10th Guards BAP			
86th SBAP		134th Guards BAP		
284th SBAP		135th Guards BAP		

2nd Guards BAK
1st Guards BAD

1941	1942	1943	1944	1945
46th SBAP		80th Guards BAP		
202nd SBAP		81st Guards BAP		
321st SBAP		82nd Guards BAP		

8th Guards BAD

1941	1942	1943	1944	1945
	780th BAP		160th Guards BAP	
	804th BAP		161st Guards BAP	
	854th BAP		162nd Guards BAP	

Reconnaissance units of Red Army Air Force

1941	1942	1943	1944	1945
	2nd RAP of GK KA	47th Guards RAP of GK KA		
40th SBAP	40th RAP of GK KA	48th Guards RAP of GK KA		
	4th RAP of GK KA	98th Guards RAP of GK KA		
32nd SBAP		32nd ORAP	99th Guards ORAP	
	366th BBAP	366th ORAP	164th Guards ORAP	
50th SBAP		50th ORAP		193rd Guards ORAP

Bomber units of Naval Aviation

1941	1942	1943	1944	1945
73rd BAP Baltic Fleet Air Force			12th Guards BAP	
34th BAP Baltic Fleet Air Force				34th G.BAP

COLOUR PLATES

1
Pe-2 of 4th GvBAP, Leningrad Front, December 1941
Pe-2 'white 22' was from the first series of 'Peshkas' delivered to the VVS RKKA, the bomber being armed with a ShKAS machine gun in the TSS-1 upper defensive mounting. The aircraft had several characteristic features synonymous with first series Pe-2s, namely the large area of the fuselage nose that was partly glazed and the glazed rear section of the 'turtle' canopy. An aircraft identical to this one was crewed in October 1941 by Sgt N A Danyushin – one of the few radio-operator/gunners to see action from the first day of the Great Patriotic War to the last. He flew 183 combat sorties, personally shot down three enemy fighters and shared in the destruction of ten more with other gunners. Danyushin was awarded the title of Hero of Soviet Union after the war.

2
Pe-2 of 128th SBAP, Kalinin Front, January 1942
Pe-2 'white 8' features a new FT upper defensive mount fitted with a 12.7-mm BK machine gun for the navigator.

3
Pe-2 of 514th BAP (later 36th GvBAP), Western Front, February 1942
This aircraft was routinely flown by Capt I V Struzhkin on bombing and reconnaissance missions during the winter of 1941-42. At that time frontline units were experiencing critical shortages of aircraft due to heavy losses, so the appearance of a Pe-2 that has been made airworthy through the combination of parts from several damaged aeroplanes was not a rarity. In this case a winter-camouflaged fuselage has been combined with engines and outer wing panels from another aircraft that had not yet been 'winterised'.

4
Pe-2 of 40th RAP (later 48th GvRAP), Ramenskoe airfield, spring 1942
Unlike the regular dive-bomber version of the Pe-2, reconnaissance 'Peshka' 'blue 7' has no underwing dive brakes, one or two cameras installed in the bomb-bay and cigar-shaped external fuel tanks under the wing centre-sections. In the spring of 1942 about half of 40th RAP's aircraft strength consisted of photo-reconnaissance Pe-2s, with the remaining machines being Pe-3 fighter reconnaissance aeroplanes.

5
Pe-2 of 2nd GvBAK HQ flight, Brig airfield, February 1945
This aircraft was flown by the commander of 2nd GvBAK Maj Gen I S Polbin. On 11 February 1945 he perished near Breslau during a combat mission from Brig airfield in this Pe-2. The aircraft's individual markings, including the red nose and engine cowlings, three-dimensional stars, Guards emblem and lion motif, were applied at the Kazan factory in which it was built, as the bomber was specifically allocated to the air corps commander on the production line.

6
Pe-2 of 73rd BAP, Baltic Fleet Air Force, December 1942
This 'red 15' participated in operations that attempted to raise the siege of Leningrad during the bitter winter of 1942-43. The aircraft is fitted with a VUB-1 upper defensive turret (with UBK 12.7 mm machine gun) and wears temporary winter camouflage.

7
Pe-2 of 12th GvBAP, Baltic Fleet Air Force, November 1944
Pe-2 'white 58' was flown by Capt A A Gnedoy during the autumn of 1944. Following the cessation of combat over the Black Sea some Pe-2 crews were transferred to the Soviet North or Baltic Sea Fleets. Amongst their number was Capt Gnedoy's crew, which had originally belonged to 40th BAP of the Black Sea Fleet Air Force. One of the best naval pilots of the war, Gnedoy was allowed to paint the inscription 'For Great Stalin!' on the fuselage of his bomber.

8
UPe-2 of 12th GvBAP, Baltic Fleet Air Force, May 1944
UPe-2 'white 4' was built as part of the last series (featuring an antenna mast on the windshield frame and individual exhaust pipe stubs) of trainers delivered to the Naval Air Forces. UPe-2 aircraft were supplied on the basis of one trainer per 10-20 combat examples, with the trainer being built last in a batch of 20 or, more rarely, ten Pe-2s.

9
Pe-2 of 2nd GvBAK HQ flight, Austria, May 1945
This was the personal Pe-2 of the commander of 2nd GvBAK, Col D T Nikishin, at war's end. Unusually, it was painted in aluminium grey overall, and it lacked a tactical number. Dmitriy Nikishin, who had previously served as an instructor at the Red Army Air Force Staff College, became the fourth, and last, commander of 2nd GvBAK during World War 2.

10
Pe-2 of 81st GvBAP, Eastern Prussia, April 1945
Pe-2 'red 4' was flown by Lt N I Gapeenok, who had started his combat career in the Kingisepp region (near Leningrad), participated in all major battles including the Kursk Salient and ended the war in Berlin. Gapeenok was flying as wingman to Gen Polbin on 11 February 1945 when the latter pilot was killed in

action. Nikolay Gapeenok completed 223 combat sorties (198 on the Pe-2), and on 27 June 1945 he was awarded the title of Hero of Soviet Union.

11

Pe-2 of 34th BAP (later 34th GvBAP), Pacific Fleet Air Force, August 1945

'Red 8' participated in air strikes against Japanese positions in Manchuria in August 1945, these attacks being amongst the last combat missions flown during World War 2.

12

Pe-3 of 47th GvRAP, Red Army Supreme Command, spring 1943

Pe-3 'white 1' was a relatively rare dual role heavy fighter/reconnaissance aeroplane of the third squadron of 47th GvRAP. Such aircraft received modifications once in frontline service, with 20 mm ShVAK cannon being installed in the nose and the navigator's cabin featuring a defensive mount fitted with a BT machine gun.

13

Pe-2 of 81st GvBAP, 2nd Ukraine Front, April 1944

'Red 4' was flown by Capt K N Mulyukin, commander of the third squadron of 81st GvBAP. Mulyukin started his career with the unit (at that time it was designated 202nd SBAP) upon its formation in October 1940, and remained with the regiment until May 1945. In October 1942 202nd SBAP became a part of 263rd BAD, which subsequently received its Guards honorary title for participating in the defence of Stalingrad. Note yellow/red colouring of the propeller hub, which was a marking unique to aircraft of the third squadron.

14

Pe-2 of 12th GvBAP, Baltic Fleet Air Force, July 1944

Pe-2 'white 01' was assigned to the commander of 12th GvBAP, Maj V I Rakov. During the second half of 1944 many of the regiment's aircraft received three-dimensional red star insignias, as well as a Guards symbol on the port side of the nose.

15

Pe-2 of 261st SBAP, Voronejscky Front, August 1943

Aircraft 'red 3' of 3rd GvBAD participated in the fierce aerial battles fought over the Kursk Salient in the summer of 1943. The Pe-2, which bears the inscription 'Forward to the West!', was flown by Capt V I Dymchenko of 261st SBAP. He eventually completed more than 200 combat sorties, including eight flights in this particular aircraft in July-August 1943.

16

Pe-2R of 47th GvRAP, Red Army Supreme Command, October 1944

A dedicated reconnaissance version of the Pe-2, 'red 4' served with the third squadron of 47th GvRAP. The aircraft bears the name 'Borisovskiy' (the regiment was honoured with this name for participation in the liberation of Borisov, after which it also received its

Guards title), a Guards emblem and the sign of the Order of the Red Banner. In October 1944 'red 4' carried out three aerial reconnaissance missions over German defensive positions in Eastern Prussia.

17

Pe-2 of 114th GvBAP, Karelian Front, summer 1944.

This aircraft was assigned to regiment CO Lt Col A N Volodin (hence the 'blue 1' on its fin) just prior to him leading his unit during the highly successful summer offensive against Finnish fortifications on the Karelian Front.

18

Pe-2 of 47th GvRAP, Red Army Supreme Command, June 1944

'Blue 2' (construction number 14/177) was assigned to 47th GvRAP during 1944, the regiment's squadrons concurrently flying missions from the Crimea all the way north to the Finnish Gulf. Its crews had to master aerial reconnaissance in all weather conditions, and from high and low altitudes.

19

Pe-2 of 125th GvBAP, Balbasovo airfield, July 1944

Aircraft 'red 89', complete with a 'Stalin's swallow' marking painted beneath the cockpit, was flown by the all-female crew of pilot Ekaterina Fedotova, navigator Klara Dubkova and radio-operator/gunner Antonina Khokhlova. Finishing the war at Grudjay airfield, in the Baltic, the crew had managed to fly this Pe-2 (construction number 14/136) throughout their time with 125th GvBAP.

20

Pe-2 of 82nd GvBAP, 2nd Ukraine Front, June 1944

'Blue 1' was a late series Pe-2, featuring individual exhaust stubs, filters on the engine carburettor intakes and blue/grey camouflage. Note the inscription 'Berlinskiy' on the nose, which was part of the official full name for the unit – 82nd Guards Berlinskiy BAP, awarded with Suvorov and Kutuzov orders. Maj A V Golitsyn was the eighth, and last, commander of the regiment.

21

Pe-2 of 140th SBAP, Tallinn region, August 1944

'White 2' was flown by Hero of the Soviet Union A P Malin, who completed 182 combat sorties in the Pe-2.

22

Pe-2 of 73rd BAP (later 12th GvBAP), Baltic Fleet Air Force, December 1943

This aircraft of 73rd BAP's second squadron was hastily camouflaged with a temporary winter scheme using paint that had a chalk base. The latter feature meant that it partially washed off when the aircraft was flown through rain, hence the bomber's well-weathered appearance

23

Pe-2 of 12th GvBAP, Baltic Fleet Air Force, summer 1944

Note that this Pe-2 has its tactical number 'yellow 39' painted on the fuselage, which was a feature unique to aircraft assigned to naval regiments. VVS RKKA Pe-2 units usually applied this number to the vertical tails of their aircraft.

24

Pe-2 of 140th SBAP, East Germany, summer 1945

Aircraft 'white 26' was assigned to Snr Lt N D Panasov. All Pe-2s assigned to 140th SBAP featured nose-art of a white bear carrying a bomb. The inscription *'Leningrad-Kenigsberg'* indicated the crew's combat history, while the yellow trim on the vertical tails meant that the aeroplane belonged to the first squadron.

25

Pe-2 of 162nd GvBAP, Ukraine, August 1943

Aircraft 'white 5', flown by Lt S A Salmin and navigator Lt V V Kolotilov, features standard green/blue camouflage. It also has a white identification band encircling the rear fuselage, this marking being applied as a visual aid to help regimental commander Lt Col L A Novikov control 162nd GvBAP's combat formation in flight.

26

Pe-2 of 162nd GvBAP, Ukraine, February 1944

This aircraft, flown by Guards Lt Matveev, was built in July 1943 by Factory No 22 in Kazan. Having survived the winter, the bomber received white stars with red outlines on the nose and propeller spinners, as well as the patriotic slogan *'Under the banner of Lenin-Stalin forward to the victory!'* on the fuselage.

27

Pe-2 of 34th GvBAP, Karelian Front, July 1944

This late series aircraft (built after the 205th series) participated in the lifting of the Leningrad siege in January 1944 and supported Soviet troops in their penetration of the Finnish defensive line in the Karelian Isthmus during the summer of that same year.

28

Pe-2 of 125th GvBAP, Balbasovo airfield, July 1944

'White 95' (construction number 7/256) took part in the highly successful *Bagration* operation during the summer of 1944. Note the bomber's quick identification stripes on the fuselage and vertical tails.

29

Pe-2 of 99th GvORAP, 2nd Baltic Front, July 1944

Assigned to 99th GvORAP, which was a part of 15th Air Army, this aircraft was one of a handful of ASh-82F radial-engined Pe-2s trialled by the unit during the summer of 1944.

30

Pe-2 of 125th GvBAP, Poland, November 1944

'White 76' was flown by the crew of pilot Jnr Lt Antonina Skoblikova and navigator Jnr Lt Zinaida Stapanova. The aircraft is camouflaged in late-war blue/grey, and its tactical number has inexplicably been repeated on the fuselage and vertical tails.

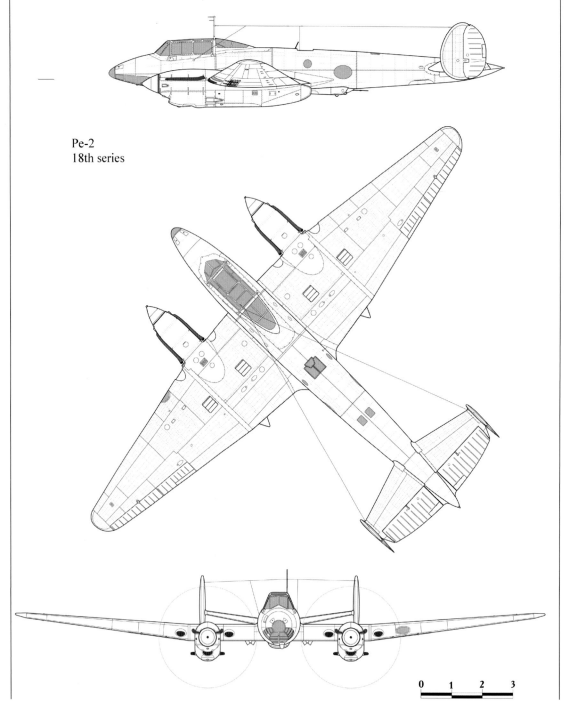

Pe-2
18th series

0   1   2   3

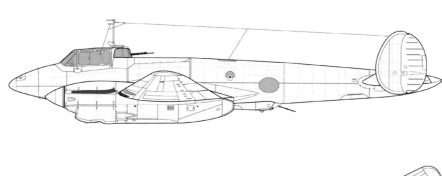

Pe-2R
based on 110th series

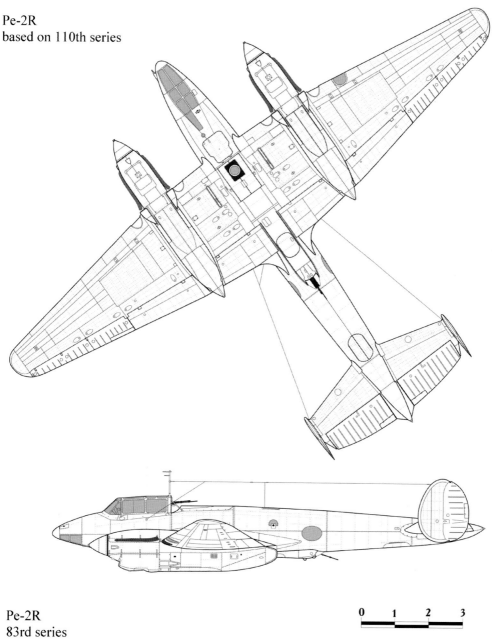

Pe-2R
83rd series

0   1   2   3

INDEX

References to illustrations are shown in **bold**.
Plates are shown with page and caption locators
in brackets.

Afonin, Lt Boris 15
Aleshin, Capt S M 21
Andre, Jacques 64
Anisimov, Capt Viktor V 18
Armashov, Capt G I 43, 44
Ayrapetov, Snr Lt Sarkis 14

Beria, Lavrentriy 8
Berlin operation 27, 68, 69
Bogutskiy, 2Lt Viktor, and crew 76
Borbov, SSgt N A 21
Boronin, Maj Ivan K 77

cameras, AFA 11, 12, **72**, 72, **73**
Chervyakov, 1Lt Vladimir 71
Chubenidze, Aleksander **83**, 84

Demchenkov, Lt Fedor **24**
dive-bombing tactics **50**, 58–59, **59**
Dobysh, Col Fedor I 13, 14, **15**, 16, 54, 55, **59**, 59;
   crew **15**
Dolina, Mariya 62
Douglas: A-20G **4**; DB-7 Boston III 53
Dubkova, Klara **60**, 92
Dubrovin, Col L A 31
Dunayevskiy, Snr Lt, and crew 68, 69
Dymchenko, Lt Col V I 31, **43**, 45, 46, 92

Fedotova, Ekaterina **60**, 92
Fedutenko, Capt Nadezhda **63**
female aircrew **60**, 61–62, **62**, **63**, 64, 76, 92, 93
Filippovich, Andrey 87–88
Finnish navy **4**, 82, **84**
French Normandie Regiment 64

Gapeenok, Capt Nikolai I 60, 91–92
Gavrilov, Maj Petr I 75
Gavrilov, Maj V Ya 56
German air force (Luftwaffe): airfields **71**, **79**;
   JG 51: 43; I./JG 52: 51; JG 54 65, **87**
German army 51, **64**; 6th Field Army 48, 49–50;
   17th Army 51
Gnedoy, Capt Aleksander A **86**, 91
Goncharuk, Lt V A 21
Gusenko, Capt Pavel Ya 58, 60
Guslev, MSgt Grigoriy 14

Kalinin, Mikhail **16**
Katkov, Maj V M **52**
Khokhlova, Antonina **60**, 92
Khryukin, Gen T T 47, 51
Khudyakov, Lt Ivan 14
Klimov, V Ya, design bureau 10
Konev, Marshal I S 60
Kosenko, 2Lt Yuriy 85
Kotlyar, Col F P 17, **18**, 18, 62, 64
Kozhevnikov, Capt Yuriy A 86
Krupin, Capt Andrey P 26, **28**
Kucherkov, Col G S **18**, 18
Kurochkin, Lt Col M A 83, 87
Kursk Salient 18, 27, 45, 56, 58, 63
Kuznetsov, Adm N G **4**, 85

Leningrad, siege of 16, 17, 21, 22, 67, 83
Liepaja 85–88
Lozenko, Lt Col P S 24, 71

Makhonko, Snr Lt **47**
Malin, A P **47**, 92: crew **47**

Mannerheim Line 22, 67–68
Markov, Maj V V 62
Martynov, Lt Col M I 31, **43**, 43
Moshkar, Leonid **83**, 84
Mulyukin, Capt Konstantin N **60**, 92

Naval Air Forces
   Baltic Fleet Air Force: BAP, 73rd **6**(34, 91),
      22(40, 93), 82–84, **83**; GvBAP, 12th **4**, **7**,
      8(35, 91), **14**(37, 92), **22**, **23**(40, 93), 84–85,
      85, 86–89, **87**
   Pacific Fleet Air Force: BAP, 34th **11**(36, 92),
      89, 89; GvBAP, 34th **11**(36, 92), 89
Nikishin, Col Dmitriy T 60, 91
Nikolayenko, 1Lt 73
NKVD, Special Technical Dept (STO) 6
Novikov, Marshal A A 30, 45, 50, 53

operations: *Arcturus* 86–88; *Bagration* 51, 65, **68**;
   Commander Rumyantsev 56–57; *Iskra* 21, 83
Orlov, Capt Konstantin 14
Osadze, Lt Irina 62

Panasov, Snr Lt N D **47**, 93
Panferova, Taisiya **62**
Petlyakov, Vladimir M, and design bureau 6–7, 8, 9
Petlyakov Pe-2: 3/25 11; 12/27 11; 13/136 **60**;
   14/177 **18**(38, 92); 19/205 10; '100' high-altitude
   fighter 7, 8; AK-1 automatic navigational
   control unit 12; design and development 7, 8;
   early series **25**, **44**, **57**, 67; engines 7, 10, **11**, 58,
   70–71, **76**; first series production **6**;
   improvements 10–11; late series **68**, **85**;
   M-82F radial-engined **11**, 70–71, **76**; PB-100
   (dive bomber) **8**, 8–9, 58; 'reconnaissance'
   11–12, **67**, **68**, 70–71, **72**, 72, **73**, **75**, **76**, **78**, **80**;
   turret, VUB-1 **10**, 10; Pe-2FT **10**, 10; Pe-2R
   16(38, 92); UPe-2 trainer **11**, **8**(35, 91)
Petlyakov Pe-3 9, **12**, **12**(36, 92), 69, 71, 72, **75**;
   Pe-3F 12; Pe-3R 12
Petrov, Maj I G 32, 44
Pimonov, Snr Sgt V S, and crew 49
Plotnikov, Capt Pavel A **60**, 60
Polbin, Maj Gen Ivan S 22, 23, **24**, 55, **56**, 57, **59**, 59,
   60, 91
Popova, Lyudmila **62**
Posudnevskiy, Kuzma **83**, 84
Prozvanchenikov, Snr Sgt 49
Punev, Timofey, and crew **25**

Rakov, Col Vasiliy I **4**, 84, **85**, 85, **88**, 92
Raskova, Maj Marina 61–62
Red Army, Air Force of the Workers' and
   Peasants' (VVS RKKA) 13; air armies 30; Army
   Air Force, 7th 15; aviation armies 53, 54; BA,
   1st 53, 54; IAP, 434th 23; RAE, 215th 71–72;
   reconnaissance regiments, frontline 73–76;
   reserve formations 30; SAP, 5th 27; RAG, 1st
   25–26; ShAD, 225th 74
   BAD: 202nd 25; 204th 30–32, 43–45; 221st 53;
      223rd 61, 62, 63; 263rd 53, 54, 55;
      270th 47–51; 285th 53, 61, 63;
      293rd 53, 54, 58
   BAK: 1st, Reserve Air Corps Supreme HQ
      54–58, 63; 2nd 61, 62–63
   BAP: 124th 65; 514th 24, **3**(33, 91); 780th 58;
      804th 58; 854th **58**, 58
   GvBAD: 1st 55, 57; 3rd 30–32, 43–46, **45**; 4th
      63–64; 5th 63; 6th 47–52; 8th 58
   GvBAK: 2nd **5**(34, 91), **9**(35, 91), 58, 59–60,
      61–65; 5th 65
   GvBAP: 4th 13–17, **15**, **1**(33, 91), 52, **59**; 5th 24;
      8th 17–18, **18**, **19**, **20**; 10th 19–20; 34th

20–22, **22**, **27**(41, 93); 35th 22–24, **24**, **56**;
   36th 24–25, **25**, **26**, **3**(33, 91); 80th 55;
   81st **10**(36, 91–92), **13**(37, 92), 55, 58;
   82nd **20**(39, 92), 55; 96th 25–27, **28**;
   114th 27–29, **29**, **17**(38, 92); 119th 55, 46; 122nd
   45, 46; 123rd **43**, 45; 125th **19**(39, 92), **28**,
   30(42, 93), **60**; 134th 51, **52**; 135th **46**, 51;
   160th 58; 161st 58, 58; 162nd **25**,
   26(41, 93), 58
GvORAP: 99th **29**(42, 93), 75–76, **76**; 164th
   76–78, **78**, **79**; 193rd 78–81
GvRAP: 47th 67–69; 47th, Supreme Command
   12(36, 92), 16, **18**(38, 92); 48th **4**(34, 91),
   69–71; 98th 71–73, **73**
ORAP: 32nd 74–75; 50th 80–81; 366th 77–78
RAP: 2nd **66**, 66–67, **67**; 4th 72–73; 40th
   4(34, 91), 70
SBAP: 2nd 31, **43**, 43, 45; 5th 17–18; 6th 31, 45;
   18-A 76–77; 31st 13–15; 32nd 74; 33rd
   19; 38th 31, 43, 45; 40th 69–70; 44th
   20–21; 46th 55; 50th 78–80; 86th 50, 51;
   94th 47; 99th 25–27, 47; 128th **2**(33, 91);
   130th 31, **32**, 43, 45; 134th 61; 137th
   27–28, 29; 140th **21**(39, 92–93), **24**(40, 93),
   47, 47–48; 150th 22–24, **24**, **56**; 202nd 55;
   204th 44; 261st 31, 32, **15**(37, 92), **44**, 44,
   45; 275th 47–48; 284th 49, 50, 51; 321st
   55; 366th 77; 587th Women's 61, 62, 64;
   608th 28–29; 797th 47–48
Red Army, Guards formations 13
Rogov, Capt A G 69, 70
Romanov, Capt, and crew **67**

Sakovnin, A A 75–76
Samokhin, Gen M I **4**, 85
Sandalov, Lt Col V A 24, 61
Savchuk, Snr Sgt **47**
Semak, Maj Pavel S **16**, 17
Shchennikov, Maj N P 74–75, 76
Shchetinin, Capt A M 28–29
ships: *Nettelbeck* 82; *Niobe* **4**, **84**, 85; *Turunmaa*
   82; *Vainamoinen* **84**, 85
Shishkin, Capt V P 58, 68
Sizov, Lt-technician T M 32
Smirnov, Capt A P 26
Solovyov, Lt Mikhail L 81
Soviet Navy 13 *see also* Naval Air Forces
Stalin, Joseph 32, 55, 73
Stalin, Col V I 23, 53
Stolnikov, Lt Nikolai 14
Struzhkin, Capt I V 24, 91
Sudets, Gen V A 53, 54, 55

Tupolev, Andrei N 6
Tupolev: ANT-25 6; ANT-40 (SB) 6;
   Tu-2 66–67
Turikov, Capt A M 26–27

Udonin, Col I D 27, 29
Ushakov, Gen V A 23, 31, 43, 62

Valentik, Lt Col Dmitriy D **46**

weapons 7, **8**, 8, 9–10, **10**, 19, **43**, **44**, 54,
   56, **77**

Yakobson, Maj A Ya 26, 47
Yatskovskiy, 2Lt S V 77–78, **78**
Yefremov, V S 19
Yegorov, Col S A 25, 26, 47, 50

Zhurkina, MSgt Nadezhda A 75
Zvontsov, Maj F F **58**, 73